WINEMAKER'S GAMBLE

The Winemaker's Gamble

How One Man and a Handful of Rebels Turned Niagara Wine into a Global Industry

JILL TROYER

Library and Archives Canada Cataloguing in Publication

Title: The winemaker's gamble: how one man and a handful of rebels turned Niagara wine into a global industry / Jill Troyer.

Names: Troyer, Jill, author.

Identifiers: Canadiana (print) 20250259125 | Canadiana (ebook) 20250259133 |

ISBN 9781771618687 (softcover) | ISBN 9781771618694 (PDF) |
ISBN 9781771618700 (EPUB) | ISBN 9781771618717 (Kindle)

Subjects: LCSH: Bosc, Paul. | LCSH: Vintners—Ontario—Niagara Peninsula—Biography. | LCSH: Wine and wine making—Ontario—Niagara Peninsula. | LCSH: Wine industry—Ontario—Niagara Peninsula. | LCGFT: Biographies.

Classific ation: LCC TP547.B67 T76 2025 | DD C 643/.20092—dc23

MOSAIC PRESS, Publishers
www.Mosaic-Press.com

Cover Design: Amy Land

Funded by the Government of Canada
Financé par le gouvernement du Canada

MOSAIC PRESS
1252 Speers Road, Units 1 & 2, Oakville, Ontario, L6L 2X4
(905) 825-2130 • info@mosaic-press.com • www.mosaic-press.com

This book is dedicated to my Dad, Warner Troyer. He gave me a dictionary for Christmas when I was seventeen, with this inscription: *Just put a few of these words together in the right order — and writing success is all yours! Love, Dad xxxx*

Preface

It's hard to imagine a time when Niagara wasn't synonymous with wine country. More than 194 wineries dot the landscape, drawing 2.6 million wine tourists each year, and generating $5.49 billion into the economy. Niagara wines routinely win prestigious international awards. Yet it wasn't always so.

As recently as the late 1970's and early 80's, Ontario wines were held in low esteem, and for good reason. They were largely made with Labrusca grapes, which are native to Ontario, and very winter hardy. While their winter survivability was an asset, the flavours in the wine they produced were very much a liability. Labrusca grapes imparted a flavour often described as "foxy", which was most unpleasant.

But something was beginning to bubble up in Niagara at that time, a revolution of sorts that became the engine that drove the evolution of the wine industry into the powerhouse that it is today.

It wasn't overnight, and it wasn't easy. It started in the vineyards, and it started with a French Algerian immigrant named Paul Bosc.

Paul fled Algeria in 1962 with his young family, forced to abandon a promising career at a large wine co-op. He defied perhaps even his own expectations and landed a job as the winemaker at Château-Gai shortly after arriving in Canada. Paul had an immensely successful career there, and his family flourished in their adopted home in Niagara. For many men, that would have been the end of the story. But not for Paul. He had a whole new life ahead, and he was ready to start all over again to build it. He was 43-years-old when he left Château-Gai to follow his heart—to follow his dream—to grow his own grapes and open his own winery.

It may have been Paul's third career, but this was his central passion.

Paul knew he couldn't do it with Labrusca grapes. He knew he had to grow the noble European varietals, such as Riesling, Chardonnay, and Pinot Noir. Unlike almost everyone else in Niagara, he believed that he could grow these vinifera grapes successfully. Paul courageously planted the first commercial vinifera vineyards in Niagara, 50 acres all at once!

A small handful of like minded rebels also started to grow vinifera around that time as well, despite the outright ridicule they endured from established growers and wineries. They all faced challenges and setbacks. But they persevered, and Paul inspired them to push on. That band of vinifera renegades planted their vineyards, and overcame endless obstacles, from weather to labour, to convincing an indifferent monopoly (the LCBO) to stock their wine. When they were at their lowest, they would look to Paul, and see that he was persisting, and finding solutions. He guided them and gave them what they needed to carry on.

Over time, their endeavours were successful, and became the bedrock upon which the current Niagara wine industry is built. Eventually, everyone hopped on the vinifera bandwagon, and quality wine became the defining norm instead of the exception. The impact and consequences were enormous. Vital infrastructure followed. Educational and research programs for the industry were established. Marketing support was developed to attract wine tourists. A revitalized geographic area emerged with a national and international reputation.

The modern wine industry in Niagara rests upon the efforts of many, but two men made a pivotal difference.

Paul Bosc was the senior statesman in the vineyard, the expert and mentor who led the way with vinifera, growing his own, and supporting others.

Donald Ziraldo of Inniskillin brought the marketing magic that made his own winery famous. He was also a tireless, and effective, promoter of the industry as a whole. Ziraldo's story is one well told, and he is deservedly recognized for his leadership in the evolution of the wine industry in Niagara.

Paul Bosc's story, while universally acknowledged within the industry, is not as widely known, though he was at the centre of the transformation that enabled the wineries of Niagara to become what they are today.

This is Paul's story, and the story of his part in the tectonic shift that would fundamentally change the wine industry. His central passion became a driving force in the central change that propelled the industry out of its doldrums and into the vibrant force that it is today.

As Paul Bosc knew, in every fibre of his being… it all starts in the vineyard.

When Paul Bosc Sr. passed away in December of 2023, I wrote an editorial for the local newspaper in Niagara-on-the-Lake, The Lake Report. *It follows here as my prelude to the telling of his story.*

Celebrating the Visionary Paul Bosc Sr. December 7, 2023

Our wine world has lost an innovator and passionate advocate with the passing of Paul Bosc. His accolades and achievements are impressive, and his legacy will live large. Behind the truly exceptional accomplishments was a truly inspirational man.

I had the great privilege of spending many an afternoon with Paul Sr. (as he is known), in the last year or so, gathering up his life story for his biography. Diminutive in stature, always dapper, and distinguished in every way, he unfolded a remarkable narrative. Forthright and fascinating, the stories flowed, often with great good humour, and enjoyment in the telling. There was no detail unremembered, no event forgotten. He had so much to be proud of, but his recounting of his many successes was very matter of fact, even understated. He was never boastful.

I came to think he must have been born with a spine of steel, because he overcame obstacle after obstacle, never even contemplating compromise. He arrived in Canada from France in 1963, as a young man still in his twenties, with his wife and son, Paul Jr. Despite the fact he didn't speak English, he landed a job as winemaker at Château-Gai. He learned English, no small feat, and built a highly successful career at Château-Gai, which included the iconic TV commercials he starred in in the 1970's. Those of a certain age will remember them, because they saturated the airwaves. That image of Paul Bosc in the vineyard, in his leather jacket and full head of hair, promoting Marechal Foch, with the tagline, "In order to make good wine, you need good grapes. At Château-Gai we know that."

Others might have rested on their laurels at that point, but not Paul Sr. There was more to come. He started his own winery, Château des Charmes, in 1978. He was determined to plant European vinifera grape varieties in his vineyards, instead of the hybrids that were being grown at the time. Everyone said it would never work. There had been experiments growing those types of grapes, such as Chardonnay, Pinot Noir, etc., but he was the first to go out on a limb and plant them on a commercial scale. He relied on his expertise from his education in France, and his hard work, and it did work. He made award winning wines, and eventually others followed suit. All of the vineyards in Niagara are now planted with vinifera grapes, with few exceptions. The grapes no one thought could grow here are now the foundation of the wine industry in Niagara.

Paul's demeanour was one of quiet confidence. He knew who he was, he knew what he had done, and he didn't need to trumpet it. So let us do that. Let's truly appreciate the gifts he brought to our vineyards and our wine industry, and celebrate him as the pioneer and true gentleman that he was.

Contents

Part One

The Long Journey from Algeria to Niagara

Flight Night

The last hour had arrived. It was a day he believed would never come, but here it was, real and irrevocable.

Paul Bosc sat on his single suitcase at a French airbase 40 kilometres from his home village of Marengo in Algeria, with his beloved dog Dukie by his side, and a dawning realization that all was lost. His wife Andrée and their one year old son Paul Jr. had been airlifted out of Algeria a month earlier. Now he waited to leave everything behind.

Everything.

His grandparents' rambling farmhouse where the family gathered so often to feast.

The Mediterranean seaside villa where he swam and laughed with his friends.

His mothers hardware store that she ran after his father died.

The town square where he had courted his wife on sultry summer nights.

The home he shared with his wife and their baby son.

The co-op winery in town where he had built a successful career at a remarkably young age.

Everything.

It was July 1, 1962, and the long and brutal Algerian war was drawing to a close. In those last days, there was panic. The rebels were in the streets, people were being kidnapped, and killing had become commonplace. Chaos and violence shaped the days and the nights.

Paul had first been told he was going to be evacuated by boat, on the freighter, but at the last minute he was told he'd be flying out of the base, the Air Force Base in Blida. So he went there, and waited for his turn. The planes were going back and forth to Marseille 24 hours a day. He sat on his suitcase. And waited.

Paul was one of more than a million so-called *Pieds-Noirs*, French nationals, who fled Algeria for France in 1962. Many of their families, like Paul's, had been in Algeria for 5 generations. As many as 90,000 Muslim Algerians, known as Harkis, left as well. They had collaborated with the French military and were no longer safe to stay.

The exodus in 1962 marked the end of more than a century of French occupation, and a long battle for independence by the Algerian National Liberation Front (*Front de libération nationale, FLN*) to reclaim it. The war started eight years earlier, in 1954. It was a brutal conflict on both sides, with the FLN mounting an escalating campaign of terror, and the French military engaging in systematic torture to repress resistance.

French President Charles de Gaulle negotiated peace with the insurgents and withdrew France's military in 1962. Political winds in France had shifted, and he had no support from voters to continue the battle to maintain France's presence in Algeria.

Day to day life for *Pieds-Noirs* in Algeria in the last few years of the war was perilous, as the FLN targeted French civilians. Movie theatres and bars were bombed, people were tortured and murdered, and women were raped.

Paul's life was restricted in many ways. He wouldn't travel anywhere at night. For six or seven years, he always put a bullet in the chamber of his gun and carried it with him. He would never go the same way to work, he would change his route every day. He trained his German shepherd Dukie, his constant companion, to be an attack dog. It was not a regular life.

When Paul and his wife had a first birthday party for Paul Jr., all the men who were there were armed. Men took turns keeping lookout on the rooftop of their house to watch for terrorists who might target the happy gathering. Social gatherings could become targets, so there was always extra vigilance. It was common to invite Harkis to join the parties, and they would help to keep everyone protected.

Paul ran the local co-op which made wine from the grapes that local farmers brought in. One morning, he arrived to find two of his workers dead. They had had their throats slit from one ear to another. It was the gruesome calling card of the FLN. The co-op hired professional bodyguards for Paul after that.

Paul, like most able bodied French men in Algeria, was part of the militia that augmented the French army. He served every weekend, going up into the mountains and scouting out rebel positions and activities.

But life was still good in many ways, and he just couldn't believe the French would leave the beautiful city of Algiers they had built, and all those beautiful vineyards, and beautiful farms. The way of life was good, and the cost of living was low.

He always thought that there was going to be an acceptable solution somewhere. He believed that because of the calibre of the French army. They'd never lost a war on the battlefield, but it turned out it was political in the end.

Sitting at the airbase that hot summer night in 1962, Paul's pre-occupation was his dog, Dukie. Everyone had been told they could bring just one suitcase with them, no more. Paul had packed his with some pictures, and his cherished books about viticulture and winemaking from his university days. And he brought Dukie, determined to find a way to take him to France with him. Dukie was just 3 years old then. Paul had taken him to the military base every week as a puppy to train him. He was an extraordinary dog, not only well trained, but he had abilities Paul had never seen in a dog. He never left Paul's side, whether on the street or in his office at the co-op.

Paul had to pay more than 100 employees at the co-op he ran, so he always had cash on hand on the appointed day when they would all come for their payments, one by one. Dukie somehow sensed that it could be a potentially dangerous situation. Without bidding from Paul, Dukie lay himself down in the doorway to the office. The door was never allowed to close as each man came to collect his cash, and then left in turn, carefully stepping over the alert German shepherd who watched their every move. There was no room for thoughts of theft.

That was just one example of how Dukie looked out for Paul during those last tense years in Algeria. He had become part of the family, and Paul couldn't imagine leaving him behind.

At the airbase that night, Paul spotted the captain, and said, "I've got my dog with me." The captain said, "Sir, we are flying people, we're not flying dogs." Paul told him the story, about how Dukie protected him all the time, which was true. He was an exceptional dog. "How much luggage are we allowed to carry with us?" Paul asked, not taking no for an answer. "40 kilos," the captain replied. "Well, then I'll leave my suitcase. My dog is 42 kilos." And Paul's friend said, "Well, I'll leave my suitcase too." So then the captain shook his head, smiled, and said "I can see how much you love your dog, but we can't fly him like this. You have to put him in a crate." Where was Paul going to get a crate! For a moment his heart sank. Then he remembered that his cousin was in the military. He asked around, and discovered his cousin was stationed at the base that night as a security guard.

Paul soon found him. Gripping his shoulders and leaning in, he exclaimed, "Jesus! You've got to get me a box!" Paul's urgency was clear, and his cousin furrowed his brow. "Let me see," said his cousin. "I haven't got a box, but I've got boards and nails and a hammer, and I could get you a saw." So right there on the base, there they were, cutting the planks to make a box for the dog. They put Dukie in the box, and then put the box and the suitcases in the belly of the plane, and the flight left for Marseille. When the plane arrived in Marseille, Paul heard Dukie barking below, so he ran to the hold. When they opened the door, the dog was loose, and Paul gathered him up.

And that's how Paul arrived in Marseille, with one suitcase, his beloved dog Dukie, and his abiding passion and deep knowledge of winemaking.

Flashback

Growing up, Paul didn't think there was anything very different about his childhood.

He was born in 1935, and he was raised in a village called Marengo, where his ancestors had arrived five generations earlier. It was in an agricultural area in northern Algeria, about 80 kilometres from the capital of Algiers. In fact, he lived in the same house they had lived in, a colonial style house with symmetrical windows and a peaked roof, in a light shade of cream. The village itself had been designed as a square, making it easy to defend. Maybe this was where he learned to be meticulous, and to like things nice and square and symmetrical. Growing up, he and his friends would go and play, and come home for lunch, and that was fine with most parents. It was an easy going atmosphere back then.

Paul spent a great deal of time on his grandparents farm in the nearby village of Marceau. They were on his mothers' side of the family. The farm was on 35 hectares, with vineyards and olive trees, cork trees and livestock. It was just beautiful. He could see deep canyons, and vineyards on the side and on the top of the mountain.

Next to the farm were thousands and thousands of acres of empty land, so he felt like he was in another world when he was there. He visited the farm on his own as often as he could, and about once a month the whole family would gather there. His grandfather had five kids, plus each of them had two or three kids so it would be a big crowd. His grandmother was a super chef. She would prepare a big feast for everyone. He loved the aromas of meat roasting and bread baking, and the hubbub of the whole family talking and the kids playing. Feasting was part of the family lifestyle. All the action was in the huge kitchen, and it was filled with mouth watering scents and the clamour of dishes. The meals were classic French meals, with lots of cream, mushrooms, often a big roast lamb. They didn't eat like that every day, but for the big family reunions, it was always a big French meal.

When Paul visited on his own, he saw his grandmother always working hard, taking care of the horses and oxen, harvesting grapes and apples. She also kept a beautiful flower garden, with roses and lavender and oleander, all kinds of flowers. He used to wonder how she did that, with all the other work that she had. His grandfather didn't work quite as much on the farm, and Paul had always thought of him as the brains of the family. He was quite well educated for those days. He played violin, he acted in the theatre, and he would go to the racetrack and race his horses there. He was a professional man. He was a blacksmith, and he made buggies. Before they had cars, and again during the war when they had no gasoline, they used horses and buggies, which was very picturesque. His grandfather had also studied how to set up the farm, and Paul later realized the arrangement of the various buildings was almost perfect, after he himself had gone to agricultural school. Paul was inspired by both his grandparents to feel deeply connected to the land, to the vineyards, and to all kinds of animals.

His own father, Armand, had been raised in a very poor family, along with some cousins on a farm. Armand's father had moved to Algeria from France. Paul's mother used to tell him that as a kid, the only clothes Armand had was a bag, a bag that they cut an opening on the sides for his arms, and a hole for his head, and that was all he wore, just like the native Algerians. On the farm he was among Algerians, and when Paul thinks of his dad's younger days, that's what stays with him. As soon as Armand turned 18, he enrolled in the French Air Force, with an ambition to become an electrician and mechanic, and that's where he got his education. He came out as a Staff Sergeant, but he wasn't interested in a military career. He just went there to be educated. So he came back into the village, and he started his own business as an electrician. He married Paul's mother Suzanne, and his business flourished. He had extremely good clientele, the very best, at all the big estates. He was a very honest man, and everybody trusted him. But Paul's father wasn't really interested in money. His mother used to tell him, she would say, "Armand, we don't have any money!" So he would say, "alright, I'll send out some invoices." He would sit down one day and write up all the invoices and send them. He was always paid, he was never chasing his money. During the war work slowed down, but he was very very ingenious. Paul remembers him rebuilding batteries. You name it, he could make it work. Paul's brother was like that too. He ended up putting a patent on some gadget and he became a millionaire later in life.

However, Paul's dad had health issues. He had very high blood pressure, which could not be controlled with medication in those days, it was back in the 1940's. He had a stroke, and a few months later, he had another stroke. And that was it. He was 46 when he died, and Paul was 11. Paul's life changed irrevocably at that time. He was sent to a boarding school. It was a very, very good school, but not a good home for a kid of 11. At the same time Paul's mother, who until then had been a housewife, decided to buy a hardware store and run it.

The next few years were like a nightmare to Paul. They were the worst days of his life. The school was very strict, and highly regimented. He had to line up for everything. For six years, he only went home every other week. It was only 40 kilometres away, and in later years he thought, "For God's sake, for 10 cents I could take the bus and go back home!" But it was the flavour of the day, to send kids to boarding school. It's not that his mother was too busy and couldn't take care of him. It's just the way it was then. Years later when he got into the army and saw the other guys complaining about what they had to do, he said, "What the hell? I mean, you guys, you can't take this?" For him the army was less regimented than his school. The whole time he was at the boarding school, he was miserable, and he just wanted to go home.

Summers at least, were good.

Paul spent summertime at the seaside. He stayed at his family's villa on the Mediterranean coastline. It wasn't that big, but he thought it was very grand at the time. Paul's great grandfather had built it, and his mother inherited it. It was on a cliff, with a beautiful view over the glittering azure sea. There was a beach at the bottom of the cliff. He often thought later, that in a place like California you would have to pay millions of dollars to have the same view. Summer days were long and languid, and life revolved around the water. He spent most of his day swimming with his friends. By 10 o'clock he was in the water, by noon he left to eat, and have a siesta, and then at 4 o'clock it was back to the beach. The beach had smooth round stones, and some patches of sand. Paul had a speedboat he loved to drive, with a 50 horsepower engine. He only had to go down some steps in the cliff and the boat was moored right there in a kind of cave. It was a good life. Not much to worry about, no one needed too much money to live, so pretty well everybody had it good. It was too good to last, he'd say in hindsight.

When Paul finally finished his six years at the boarding school, he hadn't fared too well academically. He did manage to get good enough grades and pass an exam to get into an agricultural school. By then he was 17. As much as he hated boarding school, he loved his year at the agricultural school. It was far away from home, about 500 kilometres. The students were pretty much free to go around as they wanted. It was still disciplined, but it was focused on self-discipline. If students didn't manage themselves well, then they would be put in their place, but they understood what was expected, and they had the freedom to be responsible for their own actions. Paul started doing quite well. He loved it there, and it showed in his marks. He wasn't at the top of the class overall, but in some subjects like viticulture he was at the top of the class. In many subjects he was fifth or sixth out of 30 or 40 students. It was general agriculture, but it specialized in viticulture and oenology, because that's what Algeria was about. Growing grapes and making wine. But they had all kinds of very interesting things growing there. Olives and oranges and grapes were the most important. The students worked in the fields, which was satisfying to Paul. He also loved the action in the cellar, making wine. When it was time for the grapes to come in, everybody was there, pitching in.

During that time in school, Paul worked for a man from the school who was making wine on several different farms. The farmers would hire him and he would get his students to run day to day activities, and visit to check on things every couple of weeks. He sent Paul to a winery in a small village in the South, where they were having problems finishing the fermentation process. Even then, Paul was already getting called on to solve problems. He was a fixer. He was able to solve the wine problem, but the man from the school arrived suddenly at the farm to pick Paul up. "You don't want to be here," he told Paul with great urgency. They left immediately. It was November 1, 1954, the day the FLN (*National Liberation Front*) declared war against the French, and they were in Medea, where the rebellion started. Paul remembered that day so clearly for the rest of his life. He was right there when the war started. From that day forward, the repercussions would affect him for years to come. They headed north right away, where the situation was less intense.

When he graduated, he had a choice. He could go to university for engineering, or go to the University of Dijon in France to continue his education in viticulture and oenology. There was no turning away from his growing passion for growing grapes and making wine. He chose Dijon.

There were two professors from Bordeaux there, who later became world famous. They were from a very old French family of scientists with pedigrees going back to Louis Pasteur. This time period was when winemaking and grape growing practices began to evolve and to embrace science. Those professors wrote books which Paul acquired. That was how he came to understand that practical experience is one thing, but you've got to know the true science in order to evolve properly. You've got to know the basics. This was a new kind of knowledge in the industry, and what Paul learned in Dijon became the bedrock of superior expertise that served him well his whole life. He didn't know it then, but that expertise would influence his entire future. Those books were with him, in his single suitcase, the night he fled Algeria.

When Paul graduated, he had to complete 18 months of military service before he could look for a permanent job, because France had conscription at the time. The war in Algeria was intensifying. At first he thought it was just an uprising, and the police would take care of it. But before he knew it, there were half a million French soldiers there. Paul assumed he would have to do his military service in Algeria, but instead he was posted in France. He had acquired the flavour of France, he loved France, and wanted to be in a French regiment. But as the Algerian war escalated, he felt an obligation to go back, to be transferred to serve in Algeria. To his surprise, he wasn't transferred. One day they asked for volunteers to go somewhere. They didn't say where. Paul thought it must be Algeria, so he volunteered out of a sense of duty. His regiment was camping in the southern part of France at the time. People had come from all over France to form a new regiment. One night they came and said, "Pack your gear, tomorrow we've got to be in Marseille on the piers." The next day, early in the morning they were in Marseille. Before the night came they were on boats and they still didn't know where they were going! They were given a letter the next day, saying they were going to Egypt. That was when Nasser nationalized the canal, the Suez Canal. It was a crisis. Paul was there for three months. He went back to France then, where he got a slip one day saying he could go home.

At that time he had spent more than the required 18 months in the military. He had served 28 months. He wasn't thinking of going back to Algeria. Algeria was his home, but his country was France. So he was thinking of getting a job in France. He started putting out feelers for work in the wine industry in France.

But then he got a letter from his mom. She wrote "You better come home as soon as you can, because there's a big job which is going to become available, at the wine co-op right in the village."

It was a very large co-op. It made 90,000 hectolitres of wine every year, which amounts to almost 12 million bottles. The grapes were grown on thousands of acres of vineyards. The co-op model had been very successful in France, and was adopted in Algeria. The farmers would bring their harvested grapes to the co-op, and it would make the wine for them. Then the farmers would come back for the wine, and they would sell it themselves. In return, the co-op kept 5 or 10 percent of their sales, to cover the winemaking costs. Paul was just 23 at the time, but he went ahead and applied for the job, as Director of that large co-op. The people doing the hiring were reluctant. It was a big job, and they felt he was too young. Paul saw things differently. He told the president, "you know what, it's funny that some people are reluctant to give me the job because I'm young, but to go in the army I wasn't too young. When I was 20 I was young, but now I'm ready, you know." He must have been convincing, because he got the job after all. But then there was some back and forth with the Director who had resigned. He decided he didn't want to quit, after all. He had just been blackmailing the co-op to bargain for a bigger salary. But that Director had made a big mistake, which Paul discovered. He had to tell the co-op President what he had found. He told him, "There's a letter from a wine merchant who warned the former director about a problem with the wine. It was a bacteria problem, and it hasn't been solved." So they told the former Director, "you wanted to go, so your resignation is final," and they confirmed Paul in the job. It was a big responsibility. It was one of the biggest and best paying jobs in the area. Once Paul took over, the quality of the wine improved. He went by the book, literally. He kept his books from his Bordeaux professors right on his desk, and became a pioneer in the evolution of oenology.

It wasn't all work for Paul in those years. There was a gazebo in the town square in Marengo. He went dancing there in the summer. The musicians were on the kiosk, and the young people danced in the square. The girls sat in the front row of seats, and the second row was the mothers and grandmothers just watching. He brought a photograph of that square with him when he fled Algeria with his one suitcase. It was there that his romance with Andrée blossomed. It wasn't without drama and even scandal, but they were very much in love, so they persevered.

Paul and Andrée had known each other growing up, they went to school together. Both Paul and Andrée had lost a parent when they were 11, which created a bond between them. For Paul, it was his father. For Andrée, it was her mother, and it was traumatic for her. Andrée was sent to live with her two Aunts after her mother died. They weren't intentionally cruel to Andrée, but they took advantage of her. As she came of age, they didn't like the idea that it was just a matter of time that they were about to lose the person who did all the laundry and most of the cooking and cleaning.

Somewhere in his twenties, Andrée caught Paul's eye in a new way. She was Spanish, with luxuriant dark hair and an exotic flair. They would seek each other out those summer nights at the pavilion. Andrée would let it be known to Paul, "oh, what are you doing this weekend? I'm going with so and so, we're all going to end up down at the kiosk to dance." And so they did.

But Andrée's aunts didn't approve of Paul. In fact, they strongly disapproved. He had a good pedigree, his family was one of the three founding families of the village of Marengo. It couldn't be that. Maybe they thought he would draw Andrée into danger. He had served in the French military, and he was a member of the militia that supplemented the French army in Algeria, which made him a target for the rebels. There had already been incidents where he had come close to death.

Andrée, however, was both clever and determined. She found another young man who was acceptable to her Aunts, and so she would leave their house in his company. One night, the guy was walking Andrée down the street. All of a sudden, Paul drove up on his motorcycle. Now, at that time Marlon Brando from the 1953 movie The Wild One had become the epitome of sexy, with his look of a white t-shirt and black leather jacket, and leather motorcycle boots. Overnight, around the world, that's how young men wanted to look, like Marlon Brando in that movie. And that's exactly how Paul looked that night. He pulled up to them, and the guy looked over at him, and Paul just said "beat it." It was a small world there and the guy would have known who Paul was and what he was capable of doing. He had none of Paul's charisma. The poor guy took off, and Paul asked Andrée to hop on, and off they went. After providing cover for Andrée, that young man eventually went back to France and became a civil servant. Andrée wanted nothing so boring for her life. Paul was a dashing guy, he'd been in the French army, he'd been to university in France, and he had a big job. Andrée and her family had never had money, so it was very important to her. She didn't have a bedroom at her Aunts'. After dinner when the dishes were cleared away, she slept on the table. That was formative for her. She believed Paul was going to be successful, in fact he already was, but more than that, she believed life with Paul would be energetic and exciting, an adventure.

Paul and Andrée were very much in love, and they were determined to be together. But Andrée's aunts never came around. In fact, they told Andrée if she didn't call off her engagement to Paul, they would throw her out on the street. It was an impossible situation. It wasn't as though Andrée could stay with a friend, all her friends were still living with their parents. At that time, young women stayed at home until they married and started their own family. No one lived on their own in between. So Andrée was in a very precarious position. That's when Paul's mother Suzanne stepped in. She reasoned that Andrée was soon to be her daughter-in-law, and the mother of her grandchildren, so she couldn't be forced to live on the street. So Suzanne took Andrée into her home. That triggered a scandal in the small town, for Andrée to be living under the same roof as Paul. Matrons in the town raised their eyebrows and told Paul's mother it wasn't right, but she stood her ground. Suzanne was a force in her own right, and became a role model to Andrée. Paul and Andrée were married in a quiet ceremony in December 1958. The war was in its third year by then, and a big event would just have been a target for terror.

They were doing very well. She was a civil servant, and she was earning a decent salary. French civil servants in Algeria made more than those working in France, and they had all kinds of advantages. Two years working in Algeria was worth 3 years in France, in terms of benefits. And Paul was very well paid. He was making three or four times what his wife made. They rented a house, and would have built something if history had transpired differently. Their first son, Paul Jr., was born in 1960, less than two years before they abruptly abandoned their life in Algeria. When that night arrived and Paul had no choice but to flee to Marseille, memories of his life in Algeria flashed through his mind like a slideshow. He knew exactly what lay behind him, but nothing of what loomed ahead.

Unwelcome in Marseille

'Que les pieds-noirs aillent se réadapter ailleurs!'

So said the mayor of Marseille in the summer of 1962, when waves of French nationals arrived in the port city from Algeria. 'The *Pieds-Noirs* should go and settle elsewhere!' exclaimed Gaston Defferre, the Mayor of Marseille, in widely reported remarks. Marseille was a city of 600,000 people. Arrivals from Algeria numbered 100,000 just in the early summer of 1962. It was a challenge, and the so-called "*Pieds-Noirs*" were not made to feel welcome.

Once Paul and Dukie arrived, they made their way north to the town where his wife and baby son had gone a month before. Most of the women and children had gone on ahead, while the men had stayed behind, waiting for a call to arms that never came. The town had managed to find room for the women and children to stay, but once the men arrived, there just wasn't any more room. There were already three women and four kids in a room there. So Paul and his family had difficulty finding proper accommodation. They did find something, in two different places he shuddered at. There was no bathroom, no nothing, just a tap. They slept on air mattresses, things like that. Conditions were almost intolerable. They stayed there for three months. They just wanted to relax, but it was funny, at night, even in France Paul couldn't stand anybody walking behind him. He would stop and let them pass. When he noticed what he was doing, he thought, "gee, what happened to me? This is not Algeria anymore." But his defensiveness had built up, and he couldn't shake it off. Years of looking over his shoulder couldn't just be switched off.

Paul had known France before that time, and he loved France. But when he went back in 1962 he saw a difference. He could feel the difference. In order for France to withdraw from Algeria, they had to build up some animosity towards the people who lived there, and Paul could feel it. He could feel it. He felt that politics had been played in order to get rid of them. The French people didn't want to lose territory, so they had to be convinced that it was no longer viable to stay in Algeria. And there was a false impression that the French nationals in Algeria were all rich, and they all had those poor natives almost as slaves. But France was making the rules, deciding how much they paid the workers. The French made the rules. So when Paul came back to France there was animosity. The French didn't look at him like he was French, and he looked at them as a bunch of bastards. It was bad blood all around. In spite of the animosity, they were still French citizens, with all the rights that any citizen had. It wasn't that they were kicking him in the butt or anything like that. He just felt that something wasn't right.

After three months of living that way, it was early autumn, and they moved north to a town in Alsace-Lorraine, where Paul's wife Andrée got a job. As a civil servant she had rights to a job in France, but no right to choose where it would be. Alsace-Lorraine is the coldest region of France, with long, cold, and snowy winters, which was not at all the climate they were accustomed to. At least there they found a nice place to live. It was expensive, but they managed because Paul had been able to get his savings out of Algeria when they fled. Andrée wasn't treated well by her co-workers, who didn't accept her as French. They thought of her as African. It all added up for Paul; the animosity, the cold climate they'd been cornered into, and the feeling they just weren't welcome in the country he used to think of as his own. It triggered his decision to move to Canada. He thought bitterly, "If I'm to be treated like a stranger in my own country, why not go abroad and be a stranger there?" Paul's brother and cousins had already made the move. He reasoned, "Well, we're in the North of France, we get snow from November to April, so what's the difference here or in Canada?" Climate was very important to him and Andrée, or so they thought. The decision was made. They weren't going to leave for several more months, so Paul wanted to find work in the meantime.

He decided not to look for a job in the wine business, because then it would be too hard for him to leave for Canada, if he had a job in his profession. He presented very well, always dapper in his dress, and refined in his speech. He quickly got a job in the textile industry. He was called "inspector d'avents", but that was just a fancy title to glorify the position. He was a salesman, selling textiles directly to large factories. The owner of the company was sympathetic to French Algerians, and he liked Paul. He had many different factories all over northern France. Paul was happy there, he was earning a good living, and they were happy with him. He always wore tailored suits, and he had a good car. He was only earning a third as much as he'd been making in Algeria, but it was still a good salary in France.

The company made cloth they sold to Citroen, for their car seats. It was premium cloth, but from time to time there were defects, and Citroen would reject it. Paul's company decided to take the cloth with defects to a secondary market, and sell it to auto body shops to use. They thought Paul was doing well, so they put him in charge of developing that market. He went to the factory to learn the whole process of how the cloth was made, and how it was dyed. While he was there, he had lunch with the man who owned the factory. A couple of days later, his direct boss, who Paul got on very well with, called him, and said "Gee, I don't know what happened there, but we have a very bad report on your attitude while you were there." Paul replied, "Sir, this is not true. Maybe they didn't think I was the right guy or something, but I certainly paid attention to everything that was said, and I learned as much as I could. If you think that I'm not the guy, I could quit." "No, no, no, no, no," his boss exclaimed. "Let me investigate, and I'll get back to you." Well, he didn't get back to Paul, and after a week or so, Paul went to see him. He said "this thing has been bothering me ever since you mentioned it. What have you discovered?" His boss said, "don't worry about it, don't worry about it, I know what happened." Paul was perturbed and still mystified. "What happened? What happened?" he asked. His boss told him, then. "The guy at the factory, he was an aide de camp to de Gaulle, so he was prejudiced against French Algerians." And Paul thought, "wow, here's this guy, he has everything. I have lost everything. But the S.O.B. still wanted to sink me even more." Paul had already made the decision he wanted to go to Canada, but that incident reinforced it. He told his wife, "I guess we need to go, because we're not going to put up with being treated this way in our own country." And his wife,

Andrée, she wasn't afraid of anything. So when the spring came they made the jump. It was May, 1963.

This time, Paul had to leave his beloved dog Dukie behind. But he left him with very good friends, who made Dukie part of their family. When they took him out in their car, it was Dukie in the front passenger seat, head out the window, enjoying the good life. So he was safe and cared for, which would not have been the case had Paul not been able to get him out of Algeria with him.

They were supposed to sail on a Canadian ship directly to Montreal, but it was under repair. Rather than wait, they took only the second voyage on a brand new boat, The SS France. They sailed from Le Havre to New York. There was time for diversions on board. Paul and Andrée love to dance together, and they won a dance contest during the voyage. Once they landed in New York, Paul and his family were put on a bus and it wound its way through the busy streets of Manhattan. The sights and sounds made a lasting impression. He thought, "wow, all those people in the street, so many people! They look like ants scurrying all around the place." He used to think that Algiers was a big big city, but he was immensely impressed with New York. It was a whole new world, literally. Once the bus got through the city, it found its way onto the highway. They drove north, to the border with Quebec.

They cleared Canadian immigration there, and then they got on a train to Montreal. Paul's Uncle Charlie was waiting for him at the station when they got off the train in Montreal. Charlie had been in Canada for a few years. After working to clear bush to build roads, he had become a successful surveyor. He called a porter for them, and they went to Charlie's house and stayed there for a few days. Paul thought, "thank God we had Charlie to help us out, and to find a place." He was relieved he and his family were not with strangers. They found a house to rent, right on the Richelieu River. It was a beautiful site. As a matter of fact, years later, he went back to see the place where they landed, so to speak. And by then, only millionaires lived there! After they left it became a beautiful bedroom community just outside Montreal.

When Paul and Andrée moved into that house in the spring of1963, they thought of it as their new home. Their second son, Stephan, was born while they lived there. They expected to settle and stay there, but fate was soon to choose a different path for Paul. They didn't know it as they unpacked their crates and arranged their furniture and met their neighbours, but their time in their new home on Richelieu River was to be much shorter than anticipated.

Finding His Way

As soon as they found their feet and moved into their new home, Paul knew he needed a job. He had about $8,000 left in savings, which was a fortune in France at that time for a young man of 28. So they didn't have any hardship. They were able to buy a fridge and whatever else they needed to get settled. But that money wouldn't last forever. He wasted no time finding work. Within a couple of days he started at the SAQ, Quebec's liquor store. It wasn't a job as an oenologist, just as a labourer. He earned $1.25 an hour. It wasn't quite enough to meet their living expenses, so they were dipping into the money they had brought with them.

His job was to decant any defective wines from their bottles. Everything went into the same big barrel, if it was a little cloudy. All the wine was mixed together in one batch, and then it was filtered and re-bottled. It got sold at a very cheap price, just 95 cents a bottle. It may have been a menial task, but Paul still harboured bigger ambitions. Paul noticed that the wine he was decanting most was a wine made by a company called Château-Gai. The name sounded French, so he asked the foreman about that. "Gee, these people at Château-Gai seem to have a lot of problems with their wine, I'm decanting a lot of them." The foreman said, "Yeah, it's down in the Niagara Peninsula, in Niagara Falls. I know their representative, his name is Bob Parent." Paul said, "Do you have his phone number?" The foreman gave Paul the phone number. He called Bob Parent, and he was speaking perfect French. He was their sales agent, based in Montreal. Paul told him he was an oenologist, and where his diploma was from in France. He said he was looking for a position as a winemaker. He couldn't tell him they had crappy wines, even though he could see they had problems with their wines. Paul just said, "When I saw Château-Gai on the label, it sounded French to me, so you're the first one I called."

Parent said he would pass Paul's information on to the head office in Toronto, and that they might be interested. Paul was thinking that in France, when they say 'I'll call you back', it means get lost. So he thought, oh well, at least I tried. But the very next day, Parent did call back. He asked Paul to come to Montreal that Thursday, to meet the Vice President of Château-Gai. And so it began, a whirlwind of events.

Paul took the day off from the SAQ. He was very excited to go and meet Parent and the Vice President. He got lost in Montreal. He didn't know his way around at all, but he still managed to get there on time, because he had built in extra time. He wanted to be there right on time. He felt it was important for making a good first impression. The Vice President didn't speak French, he was a very British sort of Canadian, a nice gentleman, with a moustache. Parent explained Paul's background to him, and showed him Paul's diploma. They were examining the diploma, and Paul said, "look, you've got the seal of the university right here." He was thinking maybe they thought he had faked it. But the meeting went well, and at the end, Parent said any decision to hire Paul would have to be made by the President, so could Paul go to Toronto to meet him? Paul agreed, but asked how he would get there. Parent said they would buy Paul a plane ticket, and arrange to have him picked up at the airport.

The last time he'd been on a plane was less than two years earlier, when it was transporting him and many others fleeing Algeria to Marseille. This time it was a completely different experience. The very next week, Paul was on an Air Canada flight from Montreal to Toronto. He was picked up at the airport by Jan Van Der Ree, who was a Dutchman who had worked for the U.N. in Paris for several years, and ended up working as the financial controller for Château-Gai. He spoke excellent French. They left the airport and got onto the highway and made their way to the city. They drove downtown, to Bay Street, the financial district of Toronto, and the financial heart of the country. Paul craned his neck and looked out the car window, peering up at the glass towers, and watching the office workers in suits with their briefcases all walking with such brisk purpose. He wouldn't be impressed by that scene today, but at the time, it was almost overwhelming.

They went together to the office of the President of Château-Gai, Alexander Sampson. Paul's first impression was that he was just a little guy. He was sitting in an armchair, and you could hardly see him. Sampson spoke excellent French, and Italian as well. He was a devout Catholic. He told Paul about the several audiences he had had with the Pope. The first thing he asked Paul was his religion. Paul was Roman Catholic, but not as devoted as Sampson. Paul thought, "This guy is a tiger, I mean, everybody is scared as hell of him." For some reason, though, Paul and he got along well right from the start. The next thing Paul knew, he was told he'd have to go to Niagara Falls, to meet the people at the winery. Van Der Ree had become Paul's guide in a way, and so they went to Niagara Falls together. They stayed at the Brock Hotel, which had a beautiful view of the Falls. Paul looked at the price of the room on the back of the door. It was $6. "Wow," he thought, "could you believe $6?!" It was a premium hotel.

The next day, he met with David Diston, who was the superintendent of the winery. They spent the whole day together, touring the production facility, and Diston was asking Paul lots of questions. His answers must have been good, because the next thing he knew, he was told he'd have to go and see the President one more time. Paul could tell, by then, that they had made up their minds, and he was their man. The only problem was that he didn't speak English. When they got back to Toronto and met with Sampson again, he told Paul he wanted to hire him, but said he couldn't go to the winery right away because of his lack of English. So he'd have to go and work at one of their stores in Toronto, and they would hire a private English teacher to work with him 2 or 3 hours a day. After three months, he could go to the plant in Niagara Falls. Paul was both delighted and a bit surprised at the speed of it all. He'd barely started his minimum wage job at the SAQ before he'd been hired to work at a big wine company! And all because he had the guts to make a phone call to a company that had a name that sounded French. On paper it sounded like too much of a long shot to ever become reality. But it was real, alright.

It was a moment in time that exemplified Andrée's willingness to support Paul's ambitions. Their lives had been upended in enormous ways. They had fled Algeria, found a rocky reception in France and sailed to North America. They had just found their feet in St. Hyacinth, not even a year earlier. Paul Jr. was three years old, Stephan just a baby. Andrée could have said, "Why don't we give Quebec a chance? I'm tired, and this looks like a really peaceful place. She could have kiboshed that move if she'd wanted to. They speak French here, we have family nearby, and you have a decent job."

But Andrée didn't say any of that. She didn't voice any objections. She did say, "Paul you make $65 a week now at the SAQ. Get those men to offer you $100 a week." Paul got the salary, and Andrée committed to moving more than 700 kilometres away, with an infant and a toddler, to one more strange place, where she would have to learn English. She did all that, and never glanced back over her shoulder.

Paul started working at the store in Toronto. Andrée and the boys stayed behind in Quebec for the time being. The store was on Yonge Street. Paul remembers there was a huge Canadian Tire store across the street. He was just cleaning, washing the windows, and putting wines on the shelves. The store manager was a Dutch guy, who had gone through the same process, in his own early days. When he came from Holland he couldn't speak English and he started the same way. Paul didn't know how many years it took him but he thought, "well, now he's the manager of the store, so geez, if I do as well as he does, I'll be doing okay." Decades later, he would laugh wryly remembering the irony of that early ambition, which he far exceeded.

There was also a young guy who worked at that store, his name was Ben. A Canadian boy. He was probably only paid a dollar and a half an hour, but Ben was sort of Paul's supervisor and he was trying to teach him some English. He had a bottle of floorwax and a cloth. Ben would say to Paul, loudly, "This is wax. Say wax." So Paul said wax. "This is cloth, cloth. Put wax on cloth." Ben continued with his exaggerated pronunciation and loud volume. "This is floor. Shine the floor." Paul had trouble containing his mirth, thinking, "that's how he's gonna teach me English, getting me to do the work that he doesn't want to do." It was hard to keep a straight face. But Paul waxed the floor, and stocked the shelves, and gradually learned more and more English. Three months later, he had a meeting with the President to check on his progress. Paul's English wasn't perfect, but it was proficient enough to have a good chat. The President said, "well, I think you're ready to go to Niagara now."

The whole process was a bit of a blur. Things had happened so quickly, but from the first day he started at the SAQ he knew he would never put up with mediocrity. He was determined to find a way to use his skills and expertise as an oenologist. He just didn't realize he would find himself in that position so soon. In less than two years, he had fled Algeria, spent three months in a village north of Marseille with his wife and baby son in squalid conditions, relocated to the north of France and worked there for several months, taken his family across the Atlantic to a new home in Quebec, and here he was, moving his wife and now two small sons to English speaking Niagara Falls. It had been a turbulent time. He certainly hadn't seen himself in Niagara Falls the night he sat on his suitcase with his dog Dukie at the French air base in Algeria, waiting his turn to board a flight to flee the fighting and chaos there.

Paul arrived at Château-Gai in Niagara Falls in the Spring of 1964. They were only three or four months away from harvest, and without a winemaker, because the previous winemaker had been fired. They needed someone, and that someone was Paul. As soon as he got there, he could see they were having problems with their wine. There was yeast growing in the wine after it was bottled. That was the reason so many bottles were cloudy, as Paul had seen when he was working at SAQ. The problem had been going on for a long time. Paul realized there were two things causing the problem. The people there didn't know that much about contamination and filtration. They were filtering the wine in a sterile way, but their line was contaminated after the filtration. They would rinse the pipeline, but they weren't sterilizing it properly. The second problem was that they were using sulphur to kill the yeast, but they weren't doing it correctly. Live yeast was getting into the bottled wine. Paul changed those two things right away. It took him a couple of months. Paul's English was still imperfect, and people who worked there would tell him all these stories. They didn't know what was wrong, they just wanted to stay out of it. But he got those two problems fixed, and that did the trick. The President, Sampson, thought Paul was a genius, to be able to resolve the issue so fast. It had been so stubborn for so long. Paul thought, "I wasn't a genius. I just knew two things!," and grinned to himself.

It turned out he knew more than two things, and there were other issues at the winery. They were bottling the wine hot at the time, at more than 50 degrees, which was a common method then. Bottling at that high temperature would kill the microorganisms in the wine. But there is also protein in wine, and if you haven't removed part of the protein, then the heat makes the protein coagulate, and you get flakes in your wine. The people who worked there told Paul they had tried everything, but they still had the problem. Paul asked them if they had checked the protein, but no one would tell him anything. He had to figure it out on his own, and he did. That's what an oenologist should know. He knew that, but no one else had realized what was causing the flakes. So he fixed that up for them too. Eventually he was put in charge of everything, including the lab. They fired a lot of people, and put Paul in charge of the lab, as well as production.

When Paul and his family first came to Niagara, they lived in a small house on Manor Drive in Niagara Falls, just off Lundy's Lane. It was the type of place that you had to keep your wits about you, and watch out for trouble. It was lower middle class at best. They lived there for four years. Then in 1968, they built a house on Waterloo Drive in Niagara Falls. It was a baby boomer subdivision. Their neighbours were doctors, hospital presidents, and entrepreneurs. Paul had only arrived in Canada five years earlier, and here he was, building a 2200 square foot brand new home in a great neighbourhood. That's where the boys grew up, and made lifelong friends. There were a few things that made that house possible. For one thing, construction costs in the 60's were $15 per square foot. The legal fee for the whole thing was only $50. At the time, Château-Gai was still a family business, and the president personally approved the loan for Paul and Andrée to build their new home. Paul paid it all back, though it took a few years. The other factor was Andrée. Unlike the other moms in the neighbourhood, Andrée went out to work. Paul had a good job at Château-Gai, but he wasn't on the same financial footing as the doctors and executives in the neighbourhood. Combining his salary with Andrée's made it possible. Andrée worked as a teacher, starting in the late 60's. She taught French. It was much more the exception than the rule that women worked outside the home at that time. Andrée didn't have a university degree then, but French teachers were in high demand. She barely spoke English, so the school thought she must be a good French teacher. The kids all called her Madame Bosc, and they adored her.

She taught in a circuit, she could be at four or five different schools in a day. She was bouncing around all day. At each school she would swoop in, making a dramatic entrance. Everyone knew Madame was in the building. She made an impression on people.

Almost everyone of a certain age who went to school in the area had French classes with Madame Bosc, and everyone remembered her, even decades later. By the time Paul Jr. was in grade four, she was his French teacher. She did eventually get her teaching certificate. She went to night school to get her Bachelor of Arts degree in Education, and two masters' degrees, and then she started working on her doctorate!

During those years, Andrée never seemed to sleep. The kids would go to bed, and she still had a lot to do to keep the household running. She and Paul had a division of labour at home. He would cut the grass and put the garbage out. Cleaning and cooking and laundry were all on her plate. In the mornings, Andrée was the first one up. She had to get herself ready for work, but she always had breakfast on the table and did whatever was needed to get the boys ready for their day. She had incredible energy. She and Paul were a match in that way. One plus one with them added up to much more than two!! More like the energy of ten!

The years went by, and life was busy but stable at last. All was well over that span of more than ten years. And then, a twist of fate.

Labatt's bought Château-Gai, and the guy who had been fired when Paul started years earlier came back to haunt him, as his new boss. "You can't make this stuff up!" he thought. "This isn't a story, it's a horror story!" The new boss wanted to fire Paul, but Paul had something going for him in addition to his excellent work and many successes. His new boss didn't realize it at first, but Paul had something up his sleeve.

This story deserves some context.

In the 1970s the ban was lifted on television advertising for wine and beer. Beer producers became massive advertisers on television. Since Château-Gai was owned by Labatt's, a big beer company, they saw the potential for advertising wine, as well as beer. They recruited J. Walter Thompson, which in the day was the most prominent advertising and marketing firm in North America. It was a very famous company. One day a bunch of J. Walter Thompson executives came to Château-Gai. They were brainstorming scenarios, trying to come up with what a TV commercial for Château-Gai wine could look like. Paul got called into that meeting because they had a technical question. They called him in as the winemaker. He walked into the boardroom. This was the early 70s. He had a full head of hair, a big moustache like the football star Joe Namath, and he'd always been a natty dresser. He liked to dress stylishly, in a leather jacket and a tie. Paul answered their questions in his French accent. The J. Walter Thompson guys all looked at each other with raised eyebrows. They said, "there's your spokesman, that Italian looking guy with the French accent! There can't be a better way to sell wine than that!" And that's how he got the gig.

That gig made Paul the face of Château-Gai. He was the star of their new commercials. Those ads ran on television around the clock. The airwaves were saturated with them. Paul was pictured in the vineyard promoting Marechal Foch, a wine made with a French hybrid grape. In the ad, he proclaimed, "in order to make good wine, you need good grapes. At Château-Gai we know that." He was a hit.

Paul's son Paul Jr. was in grade nine or grade 10 at the time. He went from being a completely anonymous kid in high school, to a minor celebrity himself because of his dad. Everybody was talking about those commercials. When the family was watching TV at home the commercials would come on every single hour. This was before cable, so everyone was watching the same few shows on CBC and CTV. The ads were on everything, even Hockey Night in Canada, with its massive audience.

At that time, Paul had a small farm in New York state on the other side of the border. When he would cross the border, the border guard would say, "Oh! You're the guy on TV!!!!" It would take longer to get across the border because the border agent wanted to talk to the celebrity. Paul was recognized everywhere in public. The ads ran for four or five years. There was a new version each year. They spoke to what was then a premium product, priced at $2.95 a bottle. Once the ads started running, sales went from 500 cases to 50,000 cases! It was a huge commercial success. One of the unintended consequences was actually to boost sales for a competitor. The ads were so successful, Château-Gai sold out of Marechal Foch. Donald Ziraldo, over at Inniskillin, wasted no time leveraging that popularity. His own Marechal Foch wine got a big sales boost.

So when the new boss with the axe to grind came back with his axe, Paul had an advantage because of his profile with the commercials and the success of the wine. He may have wanted to fire Paul, but Paul knew that because he was making commercials for Château-Gai wines, and he was on TV all the time, he was safe. Even the President of Labatt's was always asking, 'How is Paul doing?' So the new boss couldn't fire him. Paul told him, "You know what? I think I could quit and get a job anywhere, anytime. But I'm not going to quit until I see you fired!" His boss's face went red, crimson red. Paul had never been one to back down or quit.

Paul had also developed a new blend, called Alpenweiss, which was exceptionally successful. The company thought they might sell 10,000 cases or so in the first year, which would have been a success. But they ended up selling 80,000 cases. It was incredible! Sure enough, eventually his new boss was fired, again. Paul had persevered, as the source of Château-Gai's panache as well as its commercial success. By then, though, Paul was in the early stages of planning for his own winery, and literally planting the seeds for the future transformation of the wine industry in Niagara. It was not in his nature to rest on his laurels. There was a new horizon beckoning. After his experiences at Château-Gai, even though he'd come out on top, he had developed an appetite to be his own boss.

Part Two

Taking the Gamble

Vinifera—Innovation and Obstacles

Paul knew that everyone thought he was crazy, they believed it couldn't be done. His was a grand ambition, but then, he wasn't one to shrink from a challenge. He had already overcome many obstacles in his life. He knew it wouldn't be easy, but he was convinced he could grow much better grapes, and make much better wine. He was armed with the expertise and experience to back up his belief.

The grapes that were grown for making wine in Ontario at the time were either hybrids, or in the family Vitis labrusca, primarily Concord grapes. Concord grapes make excellent jelly to go on your peanut butter sandwich. They most certainly do not make great wine.

The most planted grapes in the world for wine are in a family of grapes called Vitis vinifera. Vinifera grapes include Chardonnay, Riesling, Pinot Noir, Merlot, Cabernet Sauvignon, and many, many more. The wines we are familiar with from Europe are made with vinifera grapes. Prevailing wisdom at the time was that vinifera grapes couldn't grow in Niagara, because the weather was too cold, and soil conditions weren't right. So no one was growing vinifera grapes on a commercial scale. But Paul had his own wisdom, and he was sure he could grow vinifera grapes in Niagara.

He had a big advantage. He came to Canada with education and expertise from France. He already knew how to grow vinifera varieties. It wasn't like he had to adapt, he already knew. So he began by experimenting, with very small plantings. While he was still at Château-Gai, making a huge commercial success with Alpenweiss, on the margins of his time he invested his own efforts and energy to get some vinifera grapes growing. He started a program where every farmer who sold to Château-Gai, with a farm in a good location, would grow at least a few rows of vinifera grapes, as an experiment.

In the meantime, he met the man who became his key business partner, Roger Gordon. Roger was a lawyer, but he was a businessman first. He recognized Paul's winemaking skills and saw opportunity. He had very good connections in the Government of Ontario. So he took care of all the red tape work to secure a licence for a winery, which was no easy feat at that time. Eventually though, he came back and said, "Okay boys, we've got a licence. When do we start? And what will we name our company?"

Paul's friend Vince Leonard said that since Italian wines were very popular right then, "maybe we should call it an Italian name, La Casa de Vino, or something like that." Paul rebutted, "if we don't find a Canadian name to call it we might as well give it a French name." He cast his mind back to that little villa that they had in Algeria, the villa on the cliff, overlooking the Mediterranean. They used to call it Villa des Charmes. Losing that villa was the one regret he had from leaving Algeria. He loved that Villa on the coast. He had an idea for a name for the company that would echo that place that he loved. But he had to check to see if it would be too hard for Anglophones to pronounce. His partner Roger was a true Anglophone. So Paul asked him, "Can you pronounce Château des Charmes?" Roger said, "yes, Château des Charmes, no problem."

Satisfied it wouldn't be too hard for English speakers to pronounce, Château des Charmes it was. It was 1978.

As soon as the licence was secured, Paul resigned from Château-Gai. He and Roger and Vince had purchased a 62 acre farm in Niagara-on-the-Lake a couple of years earlier, which became their first vineyard. That's where they started the winery. As they had planted the vineyards before they got the licence for the winery, they had a head start. New vineyards need three to five years before the grapes can be harvested to make wine.

When Paul resigned, Donald Triggs was in charge of the Canadian wine division at Château-Gai, and he asked Paul to stay on while he was setting up his own winery. Triggs said, "Well, I can't stop you from going out on your own. If you were going to another company, I would make an effort to keep you here, but I understand if you're going on your own. But would you be willing to still work for us? We'll pay you full time. And you don't have to be here the full day. But you have to be here every day to check things out." Paul thought that was a good arrangement for his transition, so he agreed.

By then, the vinifera vines he had asked the farmers to plant in a few rows here and there were beginning to produce a viable crop, with a lot of grapes. He had as many as 200 farmers participating, since he had had a very good response. All those grapes were coming into production and Triggs didn't quite know what to do with them. So Paul made a deal that he would get part of the crop, and Triggs asked him to make the wine for Château-Gai from the other half of those grapes. Paul made the wine, and split it, and that was the deal for two or three years.

That wine turned out to be a catalyst to bolster Paul's confidence in his grand plans to grow vinifera grapes in his own vineyards. His experience and expertise told him it would work, but he got a welcome boost from an unexpected quarter all because of that first wine made from those early vinifera grapes.

Michael Vaughan was the wine writer for *The Globe and Mail* newspaper at the time, and very influential. He had been a vociferous critic of the Ontario wine industry. He never had anything nice to say about Niagara wines. To be fair, there was very little nice to say about the wines of that time. But then Vaughan heard about these wines Paul was making with vinifera grapes, and he tried them. Vaughan decided to take two of those wines to a prestigious wine writers conference in New York City. He went out on a limb. Those wines could have been slaughtered. But he was convinced they were good. It could have backfired very badly, but the wines were excellent. They did extremely well. They were one of the hits of the conference, and articles appeared in something like 19 U.S. states. Vaughan himself wrote them up too. He said, "Paul Bosc is making excellent wine from vinifera, why can't others do that?" Labatt's and Château-Gai were thrilled. Paul was encouraged by the response of all those wine experts in New York. He was more convinced than ever he was on the right track.

Eventually Triggs left Château-Gai, on his way to eventually co-launch the Jackson-Triggs wine brand, and build what would become the largest winery business in Canada. The new leaders told Paul they preferred wines made by their own winemakers, and so the arrangement for Paul to continue working with Château-Gai came to an end. By then, Paul's own vineyards had come into production. He was ready to focus solely on his own enterprise, Château des Charmes.

The Early Years

It was a modest beginning. They built a corrugated steel Quonset hut, which Paul himself acknowledged was a very bad looking building. He knew they would have to build a real warehouse, and he envisioned building a Château in the future. In those early years though, Quonset hut it was. Paul's wife Andrée would set up a table with a checked tablecloth and chairs by the road beside the vineyards on the weekends and do tastings for any who came by. It was a far cry and many years from the sophisticated Château that would one day rise on York Road.

Those years were filled with challenges, a few high points, and endless hard work. Paul was juggling a lot. He was growing the grapes, making the wine, selling the wine, and running his own nursery. In the vineyards, the biggest issues were managing through the weather extremes and getting reliable labour. Government bureaucracy made it very difficult for Paul to import some of the grapes he wanted to plant. Decades later, when he looked back on those years, he shook his head in wonder. He just didn't know how he had done it all. He certainly never wasted any time. From the moment his feet hit the floor early each morning until he went to bed late each night, never an hour, never a minute, was wasted.

In the Vineyard

While there had been experiments, Paul was the first person to plant vineyards in Niagara with 100% vinifera grapes on a commercial scale. He was confident they would grow well and make superior wine, but the vineyards were not without challenges. He used a range of viticulture techniques to help the vines thrive, and eventually found an innovative solution to frost and extreme cold that became a game changer for the whole industry in Niagara. Paul was willing to take the gamble, willing to experiment and willing too, to fail, and learn from the experience.

Paul planted mostly Burgundian varieties. Chardonnay, Pinot Noir, and Aligote. He also planted Riesling, and found that it flourished in Niagara. He didn't believe too much in Cabernet Sauvignon and Cabernet Franc at the time, but he planted a few to start, and eventually more. Gamay Noir would come later.

The vines came from France at first, and Paul was doing his own grafting. The vines had to be grafted onto specific North American rootstock to make them resistant to phylloxera, a microscopic pest in the soil that would destroy the roots of the vines. He grafted up to 300,000 vines, planting what he needed, and selling the rest. It was nerve wracking! As if he didn't have enough to worry about, he was in the nursery business as well, and doing it all himself. But he made some good money with the nursery. It helped with the financing and running of the winery.

Winters in Niagara are typically milder than other parts of Ontario. It's in a micro climate, surrounded by two great lakes and the escarpment, with moderating winds that keep it relatively warmer. Winters in Niagara are unpredictable though, and the temperatures can certainly plunge to levels that imperil grape vines. Paul used an arsenal of techniques to mitigate against potential damage from severe cold. He used pruning techniques to leave more buds than he needed on the vines over the winter, as a sort of insurance policy against severe cold or late frost. Once spring rolled around and he could see how many had survived, only then would he remove the ones he didn't need. He was planting more and more vineyards as the company expanded, and he began to get very worried. He had no protection against an extreme winter. He could potentially be wiped out overnight. Back then, it cost $20,000 or $30,000 an acre to re-plant. Multiply that by almost 300 acres, and the number gets very big very fast.

So he started hilling soil high around the vines, covering the buds for the winter. But that didn't work out, as the buds rotted and died. Even though that technique had been used elsewhere, he decided to forget about burying the vines and grow the grapes the normal way. But still, he was very worried. He wondered if genetic engineering could give grapes more winter hardiness. It was a hot topic in those days. He visited a number of universities, and in the end, started working with a program in Guelph. They experimented on ways to make the vines more cold hardy. Then-Premier of Ontario Mike Harris came and planted the first vine, and it got a lot of publicity. But eventually the publicity wasn't positive anymore. People attacked the practice as public opinion shifted against genetic modification. It was still very experimental. The professor in Guelph he had been working with left to pursue a career with Monsanto in the U.S. Another professor took over, but at the end of the year there were no results. Plus, the program was expensive, costing $250,000 a year. So Paul cancelled it.

His next thought was that he'd have to solve the problem mechanically. There must be some kind of system. He knew from his studies in France that when you get a frost, the first few feet up from ground level are much lower in temperature than higher up, if there is no wind. The coldest air is heavy and pools on the ground. Way back then in the vineyard they were flying small airplanes to create wind. Bush pilots would fly over the vineyard and swoop down, and up and down and up and down. It disturbed the air enough to mix it up and push relatively warmer air around the vines. Those planes did the job but there were electrical poles and trees which got in the way and made it difficult. Paul had gotten to know Rudy Hafer at Niagara Helicopter. One day he said to him, "Rudy, would you fly a helicopter over my vineyard?" Rudy said "Yeah, I sure will!"

So that's what happened. Rudy flew a helicopter over the vineyard in the Spring, when a late frost threatened the emerging buds on the vines. That was much better than the plane. The helicopter went up and in an instant the temperature on the ground went from -2C to +3C. Paul thought, what about if we do it in winter? So he asked Rudy, "Could you fly at night?" Rudy said "Yeah, I can definitely fly at night." Paul said "I want to do it in the winter." So they did it that winter. When it was -10C at the top of the vines, and -20C at the bottom, the helicopter flew over, and the temperature on the ground instantly went up by eight degrees. Paul marvelled, "Wow! Seven, eight degrees, you have to see it to believe it!"

It may have been magical, but it came at great cost. Back then, it cost $1,500 an hour to get the helicopter in the air. In the Spring it might just be needed to fly for an hour or two to manage a late frost. But in the winter, it might be needed from five o'clock in the afternoon, until eight the next morning. And that could happen a few times in one winter. So it would have been just too much money.

Pruning techniques weren't enough, hilling up the soil too high killed the buds, scientific solutions had failed, airplanes were not practical, and helicopters cost too much money. Another person might have been discouraged. Not Paul. Never one to give up, he found another idea to work on.

Paul knew a farmer named Tom Davis, who had made a tower with a small engine and a small propeller. He made it work as a fan, but it didn't cover a very big area. Paul thought, we have to find somebody else who could do that sort of thing, but better. Sure enough, in California and Washington State, he discovered two manufacturers who were doing just that. Paul went to see them a couple of times and decided right then this was be the machine he would buy. He made the deal with them, and ended up buying 31 fans, at a cost of a million dollars. One million dollars was a lot of money to lay on the line. As fate would have it, the next winter was mild, and the fans weren't needed. Those fans were the talk of the town. People started laughing at him for spending that much money for nothing. The winter after that was mild as well, and everyone thought Paul had made a big mistake. But the following winter, there was severe cold, and the region got hit hard. Paul's vineyards pulled through with the help of his 31 fans, but everyone else was wiped out. That was when Jack Hernder, who had a winery in the area, became the second person in Niagara to buy those fans. Someone asked him if he'd done enough research to know if they worked. He said, "No, not really. What I've done is just look around and I see my neighbour's vineyards, and he's got no damage, and my vineyard is killed, almost right down to the ground. That's my research! He's got machines that I haven't got, and I'm getting some."

Paul never lost a crop after he installed the fans. Others could see that, but the fans were expensive, so they were hesitant. It would be a huge investment. The banks were starting to wonder if the fans would be worthwhile, to mitigate the risk of extreme winters. Matthias Oppenlaender was an experienced grower, and his bank manager knew that Matthias knew Paul. So the bank manager called Oppenlaender to ask him to arrange a meeting with Paul, to learn more about the fans. The bank wanted to know if it was worth financing the fans for their customers. Paul took the time to show them around. It was in 2005. Three bankers came that day, and they toured around. Other vineyards had lost everything, but when they got to Paul's vineyards on York Road, he had a full crop. He hadn't skipped a beat. The bankers had their answer.

From those first 31 fans that Paul put his money down on, the number grew to more than 600 in Niagara. They are credited with making grape growing sustainable in the regions' unpredictable deep freezes. It wasn't the first time he had the last laugh after climbing out on a limb. Paul didn't listen to what others thought when he planted vinifera, when he bought land on York road, or when he bought fans for his vineyards. He had a quiet, but determined kind of confidence.

Labour Pains

It was very hard in the vineyards in the beginning, because Paul didn't have any labour. By then his oldest son Paul Jr. was in high school and he worked hard in the vineyard. He also recruited some of his friends and some neighbours pitched in too. But for sure that wasn't enough for all the work to be done. The vineyards needed pruning in the winter, trellising in the spring, leaf trimming all summer, weeding, monitoring the grapes, and picking the grapes. It wasn't quite year round, but it was much more than the two months that students had off for their summer vacation.

There was a guest worker program in place that allowed workers from other countries like Jamaica and Mexico to come to Canada to work on farms. Paul didn't use that program, because he was reading in the newspaper that Canada had an unemployment rate of 7%, so he didn't want to import labour. He wanted to give the work to Canadians. So he went to St. Catharines to pick up workers. It was called the farm labour pool. Paul went there with his van before daybreak, and picked up five, six, sometimes ten guys.

It was a nightmare. Sometimes he was picking up people who hadn't slept, who were still drunk. They were transient workers, drifters. There was no expectation they would be back the next day. Paul paid them cash at the end of each day. He was so disgusted he enlisted Paul Jr., who was just 18, to drive the van to pick up the workers. The smell in the van was putrid. It was an eye opening experience for Paul Jr. The guys would often fight. One time there was a woman trying to get into the van. She had been gashed by her 'old man'. There was blood caked all over her face. Paul Jr. refused to let her get in and told her to go to the hospital and get stitches. She said, "I don't need to get stitches. I need to make some money." The people that did work, rarely came back. Three days in a row would be a record. Some of them quit after two hours, and wanted a ride back to St. Catharines. Paul Jr. refused, so they walked.

Once there was one guy, and at 4:30 in the afternoon he told Paul that he was quitting. Paul said, "why would you quit now, in an hour we're going to take you back." "No, no, I've had enough," the guy said. "Okay," said Paul, "you can go." When he drove the others back at 5:30 he saw that guy on the road, hitchhiking. Another day, one of the guys wanted to go home and he was drunk. Paul thought, "oh oh, he must have stolen some of my wine." So he went through the vineyard, and looked around, and he found a bottle alright. He grabbed the bottle and looked at it. It wasn't his wine, it was a wine from Brights. He just laughed. It was crap wine. Insult to injury.

Paul actually thought at the time of quitting farming because of the rocky start he had trying to get workers. But eventually he decided to bring in workers from Mexico, and everything changed. He started with five workers, and it eventually grew to a crew of 35. Most of the workers returned season after season. They became very skilled in the vineyards. The vines were in good hands. The income they men earned here paid significant dividends back at home. Several put their children through university. Two of the workers invested in getting electricity infrastructure for their village. They became a tight knit team. They took pride in their work in the vineyards and the cellar.

Bureaucratic Barriers

Paul had to make frequent trips to Ottawa to visit the Department of Agriculture. He had to get approval anytime he wanted to import a new kind of vine. One time, he wanted to bring in some Gamay Beaujolais vines. It was a very popular variety in France, so Paul wanted to grow it in Niagara. He'd recently spoken with Donald Ziraldo at Inniskillin, who said he was also importing some vines from France. Paul went to the office in Ottawa, and explained what he wanted to do. Right away the response was "Well, you know, it's very difficult." The official opened a file and just stared at it, not engaging in the discussion. Paul looked over at it. T he file sat on the desk between them. He realized he could read the document in it. It was a list of what Ziraldo was importing, and it was stamped "Approved." At the end of the meeting, Paul asked, "Well, is that a yes or a no for me?" The bureaucrat shook his head, saying "it's impossible, there are so many things we need to look into." Paul was sitting in that office, and he couldn't contain himself. He said, "Did you go through this process with Ziraldo? I can see right here that his list has been approved!" He pointed to the file. The bureaucrat was taken aback, and he snapped the file shut. Finally he told Paul, "Well, maybe under certain conditions we might eventually approve your request." Paul left empty handed that day, with no assurance of approval in the future.

That wasn't the end of it. Paul knew from past experience he might have to make several trips to plead his case before he got approval. A few weeks later, he got on a plane to go back to Ottawa and try again. When he boarded the flight, he recognized someone he knew from Niagara Falls, who had become a senior aide to the Minister of Agriculture. This aide knew Paul, and knew what he had achieved in the industry. Once they exchanged greetings, the aide asked Paul why he was going to Ottawa. Paul said, "you know what, I've got some problems and I'm on my way up there to see if they can be resolved." Paul told him the whole story, and the aide said, "That can't be so!" Paul said, "It's easy for you to find out, go and check who's got a permit. I saw it with my own eyes." The aide replied, "hold on here, if this is true, the minister will intervene for you." And that's how Paul got approval to import Gamay Beaujolais. The minister intervened and said to the Department of Agriculture, "Let him bring it in. He's saying it has no virus on it. You're saying it could possibly have a virus. So let him bring it in, and if we find any virus, then they'll have to pull it out." Paul agreed, saying "Sure. I don't want to propagate something with a virus." He planted an acre or two, and the vines grew really well. The department never even came to take a sample. Gamay Beaujolais, as it was called then, became known as Gamay Noir. It became one of Niagara's signature wines, because the grapes grow so well, and the wines are so delicious.

In fact, once Paul started growing Gamay, he discovered and got recognition for a unique clone. He was always in the vineyard, and one day he noticed that one of his Gamay vines looked different from the rest. It grew taller and more upright. Sure enough, once the grapes appeared and ripened, they were different too. The skins were thicker and the berries rounder, with more intense colour. Paul propagated and planted more vines from that one plant. When he had enough grapes to make wine, it tasted different too. It was bolder, spicier, more complex than the others and deeper in colour. After genetic testing it was confirmed to be a unique clone. Château des Charmes was granted International Plant Breeders Rights, and is the only producer that can grow that Gamay. It's called Gamay Noir 'Droit', because in French, droit means tall, or upright. Gamay Noir 'Droit' has been an honoured part of the portfolio at Château des Charmes ever since.

The Vineyard Rebels

In the 70's and 80's while Paul was tending his young vinifera vineyards, the landscape of the wine industry was dominated by 6 large companies who had no interest in vinifera; Andrés,

Barnes, Brights, Chateâu-Gai, Jordan, and London. They made high volume wines with Labrusca varieties and hybrids, typically blended with international wines. International blends accounted for 80% of Ontario wine sales at that time. Brights and Château-Gai had experimented with vinifera, but remained focused on maintaining their market share making wine from hybrid grapes. Andrés had hit a home run with Baby Duck and was running with it. Baby Duck was everyone's cheap party wine, bubbly and sweet, made with winter-hardy Labrusca grapes. In 1975 it represented a whopping 25% of all wine sales in Ontario, and it remained popular through the 80's.

But there was a renegade band of like minded innovators perceptive enough to believe vinifera was the way of the future. They were unsupported by conventional wisdom or established institutions, but they were determined to grow vinifera grapes and make quality wines. Paul was in the vanguard, the elder statesman among them, the one they went to with questions or advice about their vineyards. He was generous in sharing his expertise, though anything he regarded as proprietary he held close to the vest, especially when it came to clones he was developing in his nursery. No one had the scientific background and discipline that he had acquired studying in Dijon and applied first in Algeria and later in Niagara. Some were immigrants from Europe who believed the conditions in Niagara were right for growing vinifera. They couldn't understand why most others were growing Labrusca grapes. They described them bluntly, as "crappy grapes that make shitty wine." They couldn't understand it because they all knew just by looking around that they had the right climate and conditions, so why were they growing Niagara and Concord grapes and making them into terrible wine? Karl Kaiser was one of those pioneers. He wasn't a wine professional, but he was Austrian. Austria is very similar to Niagara climate-wise, so he reasoned vinifera should grow in Niagara too. He and Donald Ziraldo were out on the vinifera limb right from the start with Inniskillin.

Some of the early innovators, like Paul Sr., and Hermann Weis who imported Riesling vines from the Mosel region of Germany, had experience in European vineyards and saw the potential in Niagara. Some had longtime family ties in the region, and others came from elsewhere in Canada. All saw opportunity in Niagara, and all had the stubborn conviction to stick with their belief in growing vinifera and making premium wine. They all knew each other, and their paths intersected frequently during that time. All of those early leaders embodied the spirit of innovation and collaboration, as well a willingness to struggle, and they all helped each other out. Three families in particular intersected closely with the Bosc family, and leaned on Paul Sr. for his advice and expertise.

Cave Spring and the Pennachetti Family

Len Pennachetti was a tall, lanky teenager when viticulture came calling. His dad had bought some land in West St. Catharines, to relocate his concrete block business from its location in Thorold. The decision was made later not to move the plant to St. Catharines. That's when Len's grandfather Guiseppe saw an opportunity. Guiseppe had immigrated to Canada from Fermo, Italy in 1914. The land in St. Catharines was an abandoned vineyard. It was a jungle of unruly canes as the vines hadn't been tended for years. But Guiseppe decided to farm it, and that was Len's introduction to viticulture. He was too young to work in his dad's concrete plant, so he went to work with his grandfather. That vineyard was right next to where the new St. Catharines hospital was eventually built.

Len's grandfather hired pruners to clean up the vines, and Len worked alongside Guiseppe doing what he could. His grandfather got the vineyard back into production, growing Concord, Niagara and Fredonia grapes. When they made wine with those grapes, they mixed it with California fruit to make it at least somewhat palatable.

Len went to Denis Morris high school in St. Catharines at that time, and he had an inspiring geography teacher. His teacher was an immigrant from Hungary. He had done a study of the microclimate in Niagara, and researched the viability of growing vitis vinifera there. He saw there was potential, with his old world perspective. He realized it was warmer in Niagara than in Hungary. They grew good wine grapes there, so why not here? That's where Len learned about the site map which had cross sections of the escarpment, and identified different zones for growing vines. It was still under development then. It was based on infrared photography shot from an airplane traveling along the corridor, along Victoria Avenue. Bobby Ziraldo, Donald Ziraldo's younger brother was in Len's class. His family had a farm in the north end of St. Catharines then. Those maps and his teacher's passion for studying the soil and the weather patterns as they pertain to growing grapes ignited something in Len. He went home and said to his dad, "Why don't we get a real site, where we could grow really good grapes, and make some serious wine?" In hindsight Len thought they must have both been delusional, but that's exactly what they did. They researched the best site to grow vinifera, and picked a plot on Cave Spring Road in Beamsville. They planted their first vinifera in 1978, and that's how Cave Spring Vineyard began.

Len's dad was a very gregarious guy, so after they bought that land, they would go around and meet people, to get their advice. They wanted to learn as much as they could. They couldn't go to Brock or Niagara College for help because the oenology and viticulture programs there came along much later. The Horticultural Research Institute of Ontario (HRIO), more commonly known as Vineland research station was the only organization, but it was the worst place to go to, as it had already decided vinifera vines weren't viable. It was very focused on Labrusca and winter hardy hybrids. So Len and his dad met with various growers in the area.

Both Paul Sr. and Donald Ziraldo became mentors to Len. He gravitated to Ziraldo first since their families were connected because they were both from Italy. They were part of the local Italian community. Len had a good relationship with Ziraldo and his partner Karl Kaiser, and Ziraldo was always there for Len.

Len's curiosity and desire to learn eventually led him to meet Paul. It was after he'd planted the family vineyard in 1978, along with his father John Sr, and his brothers John Jr. and Tom. It was the same year Paul planted his vineyard at his Creek Road Farm. Len didn't know him then, but there was literally a grapevine communication network in the late 70's and 80's. The vinifera rebels knew about each other and what they were doing. They were almost furtive. They didn't want to admit to conventional growers what they were up to, because they would be scorned and ridiculed for taking unreasonable risks that were beyond the pale.

Len had heard about Paul. He wasn't the only one growing vinifera, but he was "the worst", so to speak. Len had just planted 12 acres, but Paul had planted 50 acres all at once, the largest planting in the province. Len was incredulous as he recognized that as a huge undertaking. He wanted to meet Paul, and it wasn't hard. The environment in Niagara at that time was like those high-tech innovation hubs, where you've got all this talent in one place, and everyone feeds off each other and learns from each other. They were competitors and colleagues at the same time.

To Len, Paul was just so unique. Unlike the other guys, who were self taught, Paul was the real deal, with his formal education and extensive experience. Len gravitated toward him, especially for viticulture. He became Len's go to guy for advice, and he also bought vines from Paul, which he had propagated in his own nursery. Len wouldn't purchase vines from anybody else because he didn't trust them in those days, but he trusted Paul. Those first vines he got from Paul thrived for more than forty years.

Len used to marvel at the perfection of Paul's vineyards every time he drove by them on Creek Road. The vines were on a perfect grid, like soldiers lined up for inspection. Len had done his best to plant his own vineyard in straight lines, but he was using old school methods and equipment. For the first vineyard he planted, he used a two wheel drive tractor. There was a bit of a slope in the field, so the tractor meandered all over the place. The rows were definitely not straight. The next time, he hired professionals to help. They were local farmers. This time, they had a four wheel drive tractor, so it could hold the line better, but it still wasn't really good. It was okay, but then he'd look at Paul's perfect vineyards again and wonder once again how the hell he did that.

It was actually a painstaking process. There wasn't any laser technology, or satellite imaging to assist planting. Paul used wires, and they pulled them taut, and marked the lines in the soil. When they went to plant a row of vines, they had a grid that was marked and accurate. They would measure the whole grid, and the exact distance between the rows, and spray paint the whole grid. Paul was a pioneer, not only in choosing the right varieties, but in knowing how to plant them with the kind of accuracy and attention to detail that was absent in agriculture in Niagara in those days. Where Paul had come from farming was a bona fide industry that had science, it had research, it had schools, it had all those things. Paul was a product of that. So in Niagara everyone was paying attention to how he did things. At least everyone in the circle of those early innovators.

There was an institutional barrier to wide scale vinifera planting then. The climate of opinion in the entrenched research community was very much in favour of labrusca and hybrid grapes. There was a strong reluctance to embrace vinifera, because the risk of winter crop loss was thought to be far too great. The prevailing wisdom was, don't even think about it. Len has two stories he loved to tell about Paul Sr. pushing back. He tells them with a fond, and remarkably accurate imitation of Pauls' French accent and idiosyncratic intonation.

The first was from the days when Paul was still at Château-Gai. There was a group gathered to taste some new wines, and to review the growth habits of the relevant vines. Some of the wine was made from hybrid grapes, some from vinifera grapes. The group's conclusion was to recommend going ahead with the hybrids, but not with the vinifera. Paul asked, somewhat incredulously, "How come you want to keep going with Vidal but not Chardonnay?" They answered, "because in the vineyard, the birds ate all the vinifera fruit, but they left the hybrid grapes alone." Paul furrowed his brow, and declared, "This is a strange country, where the birds, they're smarter than the people!" Len can't help but chuckle when he tells that story.

The other story concerned some research done by the Horticultural Research Institute at Vineland. There was a bit of a buzz based on the very early experiments. Brights had planted some Chardonnay, Riesling, and Gewurztraminer, and Paul's small-scale vinifera plantings at Château-Gai were underway too. So the Vineland research station, however reluctantly, decided to conduct an experiment of its own with vinifera vines. This was before any major plantings took place. It used that experiment for some time to explain its negative position on vinifera.

Paul and some of his contemporaries attended a presentation about that research. The researcher firmly stated her recommendation not to grow vinifera, but to focus on hybrids. She was adamant that vinifera vines were not viable in Niagara. Her argument was bolstered by research, from when they had planted Chardonnay as an experiment. Based on that, the conclusion was definitive: "don't grow vinifera".

Paul, with his own science background, asked the researcher in his gruff, gravelly voice, "How did you arrive at that conclusion?" The researcher answered with great confidence. "We planted the vines and 66.6 percent of the vines died." Nonplussed, Paul asked, "How many vines did you plant?" The answer came, "Three vines." Paul didn't have to say anything else. He rolled his eyes, and the cadre of vinifera believers in attendance had to hide their smirks in an effort to be polite.

Those early pioneers were proved right over time, but their journey was not without bumps in the road. Len had planted his family's vineyard in 1978. In 1980 he had a glorious crop. It was beautiful. He felt they had demonstrated, beyond the shadow of a doubt, that they could grow vinifera, and their gamble had paid off. Then came the winter of 1981. On Christmas Day, then again in January, the temperatures plunged to a frigid bone-chilling minus

26C. The vines were severely damaged. Len called it the Christmas Massacre. It made him think twice. He'd used real money, made big investments to get where he was. That winter seemed to put it all in jeopardy. In those times of uncertainty, it was so important to have a guy like Paul to talk the way he did, with all his training, and scientific discipline. He had eyes wide open about the risk, but he still had the conviction vinifera would work. Len and others like him needed people like Paul to give them the confidence to carry on. Len's friend Ziraldo helped him through that time as well. The vines produced nothing the following season. Len feared they were lost. Ziraldo came and walked Len's vineyard with him. He reassured him the vines were still alive. They would produce grapes in the next season.

Len spent many an enjoyable evening in the Bosc family home over dinner and lots of conversation. That was when he first met Paul Jr., who became a lifelong friend, and his younger brother Stephan. Len and his girlfriend Helen (they were later married) would visit at the Bosc home in Niagara Falls, in the house Paul Sr. had built in a prosperous suburban neighbourhood when he was still at Château-Gai. Later, Len and Helen would visit them in the house they moved into when Paul Sr. started his winery. It was on the property on Creek Road where the winery was, and it was considerably more modest than their earlier home in Niagara Falls. To Len, it reinforced Paul and Andrée's commitment and willingness to make sacrifices to build his winery.

Len knew the viticulturist at Brights Wines, the biggest winery in Niagara at the time. He was talking to him once, and he told Len with scorn just what he thought of Paul's first two sites. "If I gave you a map and asked you to point out the worst two sites in all of Niagara-on-the-Lake to plant vinifera, his two sites would be what I would have chosen."

To Len, that made Paul's success there even more remarkable. He saw Paul Sr. as someone who believed in the art of the possible. He was an immigrant who came here with next to nothing, and he did well despite the naysayers. The vines on those so-called worst sites thrived for decades to prove Paul right.

Henry of Pelham and the Speck Family

There had never been a family plan to grow grapes, never mind build a winery, but that's exactly what happened.

Paul Speck and his brothers Daniel and Matt were raised in Toronto, where their father was a teacher. Their family had deep roots in the Niagara region going back to 1842. When one of the last remaining parcels of land that had been in the family since then was severed and made available for sale in 1982, Paul's dad bought it from his cousin at an inexpensive price. He wanted to keep it in the family. He had grown up there. He had memories of square dancing in the Inn that was there, and visiting his grandmother across the road.

A couple of years later, he had the idea to plant a small vineyard. Paul was the only one of his brothers who could drive at the time. So Paul drove himself, and his brothers to Pelham. They planted the vineyard by hand, with help from their uncle and cousins who live nearby. Paul remembers meeting Paul Bosc back then, when they were just planting that first vineyard. Paul's father was an educator, he wasn't a farmer or a winemaker. He didn't know what he was doing. Paul and his dad would go around to meet with more established growers. They'd sit on a picnic bench and chat. His dad was trying to learn what to plant, and he took whatever advice he could get. The leaders at that time were Château des Charmes and Inniskillin, so those were the most obvious places to go. They were both very collegial about helping.

Soon after, Paul was in university and his brothers were in high school. They all came back and worked on the vineyards in the summertime and on weekends. Eventually his dad decided he wanted to start a small winery, so they built a 5000 square foot tin barn. Paul's dad was still teaching in Toronto, but he thought when he retired he'd like to have a little winery business. Paul had been studying western philosophy. When he graduated, he was a bit tired of school, so he agreed to take a year to help his dad get the winery going. They hired a winemaker, Rob Summers from Hillebrand, and they had one farmhand. Their first vintage was 1988. The doors of the winery opened in 1989, and that was the beginning of Henry of Pelham. They had produced 1,400 cases of Chardonnay, Riesling and Baco Noir. Paul was by no means planning on staying. He was looking at writing the entrance exam for law school. Paul thought the wine industry was a nightmare, and with the advent of Free Trade, disaster seemed all but certain. The first wine review they got from Tony Aspler, the wine critic for *The Toronto Star*, focused less on their wines and more on how brave (or insane?) they were to open a winery when Free Trade was looming. Paul was thinking prospects were dim. By then, though, his dad had gotten in over his head financially. That became the main motivator for Paul to stay and get things sorted. Part of him was terrified, but part of him was excited about staying. He was young and had lots of energy.

Paul's dad was unfortunately ill by then, so Paul had to take over right out of the gate. His brothers were studying classical philosophy as he had. They came out to help during the summers. When his brother Matt graduated in 1992, Paul asked him to give him a year to help out, then he could go and get a "real" job. Matt agreed, and then stayed on permanently. Their dad sadly passed away in 1993. His brother Daniel graduated in 1996. He stayed on at the winery too, after his first year helping out.

The work was never ending, and the weather was always a worry, but that wasn't all. None of the pioneering wineries was particularly profitable. Financially speaking, the wolf was never far from the door. Henry of Pelham didn't even break even until 1992, four years after their first vintage. That just meant they stopped losing money, not that they were making money. They were still having trouble getting conventional financing. Their loans were through a merchant banker, with interest rates at a whopping 23%. Finally in 1996 Paul was able to convince Farm Credit to take on their debt, and he thought, "ok, phew, now we're rolling. We got this."

Paul Bosc was a big help during that time. Paul Speck and his brothers learned a tremendous amount from him. He could be a gruff character, but he was a true gentleman. If he respected you, he would give you his time. They would walk the vineyard together, and they'd ask him first before planting anything new. Paul was way ahead of everybody in terms of viticulture.

Paul Speck remembers seeing wind machines in Paul Bosc's vineyards, the first ones in the region. He thought, "wow, that makes so much sense". He couldn't afford to buy his own right away, but as soon as he could he bought the exact same ones.

His brother Matt, who ultimately ran the family vineyard, thought of Paul Bosc as the greatest viticulturist certainly in Canada for his whole life. His vineyards stood as testament to that, always beautiful, in perfect order, and state of the art.

Vineland Estates and the Schmidt Family

The Schmidt family had close ties to the Bosc family across two generations, and their relationship was cemented during those days of risk and innovation in the 1980's. Lloyd Schmidt and Paul Sr. were close colleagues. Schmidt worked for Paul Sr. as a viticulturist at Château des Charmes for several years. Paul Jr. and Lloyd's son Allan were both born the same year, and became the best of friends. Their relationships were anchored in vinifera grapes and great wines.

Just as Paul Sr.'s passion for growing grapes and winemaking went back several generations, the Schmidts too had deep viticultural roots. Lloyd Schmidts' father planted one of the first vineyards in Summerland, BC, in the late 1930's. Lloyd was born on that farm. His sons Allan and Brian were born there too. Lloyd was a partner in the start up of Sumac Ridge winery there in the late 1970's.

Allan and Brian grew up in the vineyard, working at the family farm and winery.

With the recession of the 1980s, Lloyd sold his share of the winery in B.C. and came to Ontario. Paul Sr. hired Lloyd to work as a viticulturist at Château des Charmes, He worked there for several years in the late 80s and early 90s. The two got along very well. They were both passionate about viticulture. That created a deep bond. They both loved the vineyard first and foremost. Eventually Lloyd established his own business importing grapevines, which became hugely successful.

Allan started at Vineland Estates as winemaker in 1987. It was owned by Hermann Weis, who was among those key leaders bringing vinifera to Niagara. Weis was a winemaker and nurseryman from the Mosel region of Germany, famed for its Riesling. He was importing Riesling vines to North America. He had bought the farm at Vineland in 1979. Weis planted 40 acres of his own Riesling clones there to demonstrate how well it could grow. The vines flourished there. Allan became General Manager after Weis sold the winery in 1992. His brother Brian joined as winemaker that same year.

Allan and Paul Jr. soon became friends. He and Paul Jr. were both working on the winery side. They would attend meetings at the Wine Council of Ontario together; they were true contemporaries. They were both directors on the board eventually. When Allan first arrived in 1987, Paul Sr. was the director. Allan was quickly impressed with how he spoke at the meetings. Paul Sr. could come across as very harsh, or rough sometimes. That may have offended some people. But whenever he had something to say, it was always worth listening to. He could come from a point of view where people hearing him would initially think, "that's crazy, it would cost too much!" But then as what he had said would sink in, they'd be thinking "Well wait a minute, that DOES make sense, I just never thought of it that way!" Paul's expertise and international knowledge of grape growing was way ahead of his contemporaries at that time. Allan couldn't imagine the industry, and its movement forward, without Paul Sr. there as a force for positive change.

Like others, Allan always admired Paul Sr.'s immaculate vineyards. Anytime Allan went to meetings in Niagara-on-the-Lake, he would alter his route to make sure he drove by the Bosc vineyard on Creek Road. Others did the same thing, to check out whatever Paul was doing. Because if Paul was doing it and you weren't, you might be doing something wrong, whether it was putting on a spray or planting a certain cover crop.

Niagara may have a Mediterranean climate in the summer, which allows the grapes to grow and ripen, but the winters were more like Siberia. Cold was always a looming threat to the survival of the vines. Paul had pioneered the use of wind machines to mitigate damage on the coldest nights, but he had another tool in his arsenal. He had done a lot of research on different rootstocks, which were grafted onto the vinifera varietals. The site of the graft was always planted just above the soil line. If the plant above that is damaged by cold, you need a new shoot to come from above the graft site, not below it, in order to bring the vine back into production. To ensure that would happen in the case of a severe winter, Paul would hill up the soil several inches around the base of each vine, every year, to protect the vine just above the graft site. It was very expensive, because it was labour intensive, so others elected not to do it. Most years, they won the bet. But every 10 years or so, a severe winter would kill 25 – 30% of the vines, and they'd have to be replanted. Not in Paul's vineyards. His damaged vines didn't have to be replaced. They had healthy new shoots that would renew the vine and produce grapes much sooner than planting new vines and waiting for them to mature. Allan realized that when you calculate the cost of replanting, and waiting four years to harvest your next crop, the cost of hilling up suddenly looks like a cheap insurance policy. Allan started to hill his vines too, and others followed suit.

Allan thought of Paul Sr. as a viticulturist first, just as his father Lloyd was, and Hermann Weis too. But Allan admired Paul Sr.'s contributions to winemaking as well. He was cutting edge in his use of French oak barrels and various winemaking techniques. The quality of his wines was always first rate. That was fully attributed to Paul, but Allan believed credit for the personality of the winery belonged fully to "Madame", as everyone called Andrée Bosc. She and Paul both had a passion for wine, but she had a personality that just drew people in. She gave the best winery tours. She spent a tremendous amount of time doing it despite working full time as a teacher, raising Paul and Stephan, and keeping the Bosc household running. Allan's wife was a wedding floral designer. Whenever she was setting up flowers for a wedding at Château des Charmes, Madame Bosc was always there, early in the morning, talking to people, making sure everything was going smoothly. She was really the Queen of the industry. She and Paul made a formidable team.

Extraordinary Women in the Vinifera Revolution

The wine industry was a male dominated environment, but there were three extraordinary women—including Madame Bosc—who were pioneers in their own rights. All three were teachers, and all three became part of the driving force behind transformation in the wine business. They each made tremendous contributions in their own ways. Madame Bosc charmed customers one by one at Château des Charmes, Debi Pratt garnered attention and appreciation for Inniskillin wines with her P.R. skills, while Donna Lailey was a stubborn pioneer in the vineyard and a tenacious advocate for quality in the boardroom.

Donna Lailey and her husband Dave lived in Toronto in the late 60's, where they were both teachers. They often visited Dave's parents, who had a fruit farm in Niagara-on-the-Lake. It was right on the parkway, across the road from the Niagara River, where it flowed fast toward Lake Ontario. There was a big white house there, with a beautiful entrance and lovely gardens. Out front grew three huge willow trees, their leaves cascading green to the ground and swaying in the wind. Out back was a pool. Donna loved it there, even though she hadn't grown up on a farm herself. She was drawn to the peaceful feeling, the tidy acres of orchards, and the river breezes. When Dave's parents were ready to give up farming in 1970, Dave and Donna bought the farm from them. Donna was ready to trade in the whistle she used in her gym classes for pruning shears and a sun hat.

They moved in, and Donna became a farmer overnight. She had always been fit and active, and she was willing to work hard. Dave was still teaching in Toronto during the week. He helped on the farm on weekends. The first year, Donna hired people to pick the cherries, and she took them to market. She made just enough to pay the workers. She called Dave and declared emphatically "We're not doing this!" She could see it wasn't a viable way to make a living. Instead, Donna decided they would plant grapes.

Out came the cherry trees and pear trees and peach trees. Donna told Dave, "I don't want to plant what everybody else is planting, why not grow what the rest of the world is growing?" She wasn't a big wine drinker, but she knew that Niagara was producing a lot of wine from Labrusca and hybrid grapes, and it wasn't very good. The rest of the wine world was growing vinifera grapes. So the first two varieties she planted were Chardonnay and Pinot Noir.

The first planting was ten rows of each. Nobody but Donna tended those vines. There was a certain way she wanted them pruned, a certain way she wanted the canopy trimmed, and a certain way she wanted to manage the yield for the best quality. There was nowhere to go to learn how to do all that. Donna learned on her own, and often got help from her near neighbour Donald Ziraldo. The experts at Vineland research insisted, "Donna, just plant French hybrids" Other growers were adamant too, that she shouldn't be trying to grow vinifera. One of her neighbours actually told her he thought she was "absolutely insane." Donna knew the winters could be rough, but she was willing to take her chances.

The work was often physically gruelling, despite Donna's fitness and strength. Dave was still teaching at the time, so Donna was the full time farmer. One late winter morning, Donna was outside pruning her vines. Icy wind was blasting off the river through the vineyard, and the temperature was frigid. Her fingers were numb, her back was aching, and she was bone weary. She finally took a break, and went inside to thaw out. She didn't think she could face another hour of that. When she turned the radio on, she heard a news report about Terry Fox running across Canada. He'd had a leg amputated, and was running to raise awareness and money for cancer research. It was the extra inspiration she needed. She thought, "If he can do that, I can do this." Donna put her tea cup in the sink, put her winter coat and boots back on, and headed out to the vineyard.

Their vinifera plantings expanded during the 80's, to take up the full 23 acres, and Donna hired workers to help. Persistence paved the way to success.

It wasn't overnight, but gradually others began to see the results. It may have been a struggle, but Donna thought, "At least I know we're growing grapes and making wine like the rest of the world."

After more than a decade of growing vinifera, the scorn that had been heaped on her turned to high praise. The Grape Growers of Ontario award a coveted Grape King title each year, to a grower who "exemplifies excellence in the vineyard." In 1991, Donna Lailey broke the mold and became the first female ever to become Grape King. The name itself conveys the expectation it would never be bestowed upon a woman, but she wore the crown with pride.

Donna's advocacy for quality extended beyond the vineyard. She was an active member of many boards and trade organizations, usually the only woman at the table. Sometimes she'd come home from a meeting and say to Dave in exasperation, "Oh, why should I bother? I feel so discouraged."

She was persistent though, because she felt strongly about the need to keep moving the industry forward, by focusing on quality. It was a time when women weren't heard easily, but Donna was outspoken, and she had credibility because of what she had done in her vineyard. Eventually even some of the men even came to see what she was doing on the farm.

Challenges in the 70's and 80's weren't limited to the vineyards. It was an uphill battle to convince consumers that there was good wine being made in Niagara. Debi Pratt was instrumental in helping turn the tide on the poor reputation Niagara wine had developed.

Debi was a teacher, and she had an abundance of natural curiosity. She was the same age as Donald Ziraldo, and they were friends. They didn't go to the same high school, but they had met through a mutual friend. St. Catharines was such a small city, people connected to each other in many different ways.

Not long after Donald teamed up with Karl Kaiser, Debi would meet up with them from time to time. She was instantly fascinated by their conversations about grape growing and winemaking and the business of it all. She didn't know anything about it, but their spirited discussions intrigued her. Debi never dreamt that she was listening to the start of a sea change in the wine industry, and certainly never imagined she would become part of it. Yet that's exactly what happened.

Debi had summers off from her teaching job. One hot afternoon early in the summer of 1975, she stopped in at Ziraldo Nurseries. Donald and Karl were using the packing shed there for their fledgling winery, Inniskillin. Donald wasn't there that day, but Marion Le Blanc was. Marion ran the office. Debi had met her before. She noticed that Marion was very busy that day. Debi said to her, "You look pretty busy, so I won't bother you. But you know, I'm home for the rest of the summer, I'm not working. So if you need any help?" Marion didn't have to be asked twice. She took her office keys out of a drawer and dropped them into Debi's hand, saying "Here. I have to go to a funeral, can you take things over for the next three days?" Debi thought she was kidding, but it was no joke. "Oh my god," she thought, "this is wild." She jumped into the deep end, answering the phone and organizing deliveries. When Donald returned that day, she said "Are you ok with this, with me helping out while Marion's away? I don't know a lot about wine." Donald told her to talk about what she did know, and to ask him or Karl for help when she needed it.

That chance encounter plus Debi's natural curiosity launched her into the world of wine. After those first three days, she helped out every summer, and on weekends during the school year. Soon she was doing tastings with customers, and her skills as an educator came in handy. She applied her teaching expertise to make the tastings meaningful. People were intimidated by wine in those days, so Debi would always start with a few questions, to make them comfortable, and to guide them. "Do you like white or red? Do you like lighter or more full bodied? Do you like fruity or dry?" Based on their answers, she would put two wines in front of them, and say "Ok, now I want you to smell these, and taste them." She always gave them two wines, so they could talk about them more easily. "Which one do you prefer?" she would ask. "Oh, I really like the aroma on this one," they'd say. "This one is fruitier than that one," they'd add. And then they had their own vocabulary, and the conversation would continue. Debi built a tremendously loyal following because people liked the format of her tastings. They always said they learned a lot. Debi knew that an educated consumer would become a loyal consumer. They came back again and again, and they would buy wine by the case.

When she wasn't winning over brand ambassadors one by one in the tasting room, Debi was masterful with the media. She knew journalists had a thirst to learn. When she and Donald held tasting events in Toronto, sometimes at the Art Gallery or the Design Exchange, it wouldn't be a party. Buyers and media alike would leave with new knowledge and greater appreciation of premium wine.

Debi also knew how to pitch a story. She knew what angle and storyline would appeal to writers. When Inniskillin won the Grand Prix d'Honneur at Vinexpo in Bordeaux, France, in 1991 for their Icewine, Debi likened it to winning a gold medal at the Olympics. People could relate to that, and it positioned Inniskillin as the underdog coming out on top. People always like to fight for the underdog. Debi's P.R. efforts maxed out media coverage after that win, and Canadian wine began to develop an identity. When she sent out a press release, there was always a human interest storyline there. Debi's press releases were never tossed in the waste basket, they were picked up for coverage.

Wintertime at the wineries was always much quieter than the summer. Debi was determined to attract more tourists in the winter months. She said to Donald and to their vineyard manager, "We're celebrating ice wine in the winter. People come, and the one thing they don't believe is that the grapes can last that long on the vine. They think we freeze them artificially or something. We keep saying they are frozen naturally on the vine, and harvested that way, but they don't believe it. What if they could see it?" She was building her case to convince them to do something they'd never done before. "What if we keep the grapes on a couple of rows of vines all winter, so people can see them, touch them, taste them?" Donald and the vineyard manager agreed, and visitors loved it. Even if all the other grapes had been harvested, they could still see the grapes on those few rows. They were fascinated. Debi would explain, "You can see why Icewine is so expensive. If you look at these bunches here you see how some of them are gradually breaking down. We only get a single drop of concentrated juice from each grape, so it takes so many more grapes to make Icewine compared to table wine." She could see the lightbulbs going off as her visitors came to understand the low yield, the concentration of sugar and flavour, and hence the higher price. It paid off for people to actually see the grapes. They gained a greater appreciation for Icewine, and it led to more sales.

Debi was an early leader at a time of transition in the industry. Her impact stretched far further. Other women followed as the industry evolved, and many of them were generously mentored by Debi.

The Rest of Team Vinifera

Inniskillin, of course, was a major player in the development of growing better grapes and making premium wines, and their history is well documented. Donald Ziraldo came from a farming family.

In addition to tender fruit they were growing hybrid grapes that were definitely an improvement on labrusca. Karl Kaiser was making wine, and he did not want to use labrusca grapes. He discovered the Ziraldo family farm, and bought hybrid vines from them. He later returned to the farm with a bottle of the wine he had made. Ziraldo and his mother tasted it. They were impressed. Not long after the two men decided to start their own winery. Ziraldo managed, against the odds, to secure a licence in 1975, and Inniskillin was born. Karl made the wine, and Ziraldo sold it with great flair and panache. Debi Pratt was their P.R. partner.

In 1978, 24 year old Albrecht Seeger, who had come to Niagara from Germany with his parents, started working for Kaiser at the winery. Seeger's family had been farming in Germany for generations. When Seeger met Ziraldo, he said "Look, I'm going to be so busy selling wine, I can't grow the grapes too. Why don't we work out a deal, and you can buy my farm." That's what happened.

One day, as a young Albrecht was working in the vineyard, planting more vinifera vines, a pickup truck pulled over, and a man got out. He was an imposing figure, six feet four inches tall, and very sure of himself. He was a local grower himself. He had been growing in Niagara for the last 10 years at the time. He strode over to Albrecht.

"Guys, what are you trying to do?," he bellowed. "It's gonna fail. You're wasting your money planting Riesling. You have to plant Labrusca, believe me!" Seeger was a laughingstock for growing vinifera back then, and not just amongst other growers. Even the specialist at Vineland research ridiculed him. He told Albrecht that "trying to grow vinifera in Niagara is like trying to grow bananas."

The scorn was also applied to other practices in the vineyard. Albrecht decided to grow a different cover crop between his rows of vines. The standard cover crop then was ryegrass. Seeger wanted to do more, and grow oilseed radish in combination with the ryegrass. It grows very fast, and puts down very deep roots, which is beneficial to the soil. That same expert from Vineland laughed at him, telling him "What a stupid idea!" Albrecht did it anyway. Paul heard about it and came to see him to learn more. He recognized it as a great practice right away. Since then, planting oilseed radish as a cover crop has become standard procedure.

Ziraldo sold Inniskillin wines to top restaurants in Toronto. He promoted it at international wine competitions including Vinexpo in 1989 where Inniskillins' Pinot Noir was well received. Their Icewine was enthused over. Two years later Kaiser's Icewine won the Grand Prix d'Honneur for the best wine in the show, putting Canadian wine on the international stage in a big way. Both Ziraldo and Kaiser were pioneers as well as mentors to others in the industry. Ziraldo promoted not just his own winery, but the industry as a whole, with great success. Ziraldo and Paul Sr. travelled in the same circles, and respected each other, although they were never close. Ziraldo was the master showman and marketer; Paul Sr. was the master viticulturist and oenologist. The two men couldn't have been more different, in physical stature, in temperament, and focus, but each was an invaluable leader in shifting the industry forward.

Hillebrand Winery was another key actor in the vinifera revolution in the '80's. First founded as Newark Winery by Joseph Pohorly in 1979, it became Hillebrand in 1983, after being purchased by two buyers from Germany. They were very supportive of the expansion of vinifera both in terms of the grapes they grew as well as the grapes they bought. Hillebrand went through a major expansion in the '80's, opening 40 retail stores and increasing production from 40,000 cases in 1982 to 400,000 cases just a few years later. Much of their volume was in international blends, but Hillebrand was also making vinifera varietals, from Pinot Noir to Chardonnay to Riesling.

Two others were key contributors to the evolution of the wine region. Both Klaus Reif and Herbert Konzelmann heralded from Germany. In both cases they came to Niagara already steeped in a passion for winemaking, from long established family wineries. They strongly believed in the concept of growing vinifera.

Herbert Konzelmann came from three generations of German winemakers. He had visited Canada and believed in the potential he saw in the emerging industry in Niagara which led to his move there. Ewald Reif's family had winemaking roots going back a dozen generations in Germany. In Niagara he started growing grapes for Inniskillin with vineyards planted in 1977. He founded Reif winery in 1982, and it was taken over by his nephew Klaus in 1987.

Most of the growers at that time grew labrusca and hybrids and sold their grapes to the big wineries, but a few growers were planting vinifera. Albrecht Seeger and Donna Lailey weren't the only ones. John Marynissen planted the first commercial Cabernet Sauvignon vines in Niagara at his estate farm in 1978, later opening a winery in 1991. Bill Lenko planted some of the first Chardonnay grapes in Ontario, and later planted Merlot and Viognier in his vineyard near Beamsville. Bill's son Daniel took over in 1999, and opened Daniel Lenko Estate Winery. In 1984, Matthias Oppenlaender with the Huebel family established Huebel Grapes Estates and were growing their own vinifera and providing services to others.

Growing the grapes was one challenge, but selling the wine, that was a struggle all of its own. The early pioneers may have been making high quality wine from high quality grapes, but it took some fierce powers of persuasion to convince consumers to try it.

Making the Sales

Château des Charmes wine was successful from the start. The first year they started making wine, they sold 3,000 cases. The second year, they sold 7,000 cases. The third year they sold 13,000 cases, and the fourth year it more than doubled to 27,000 cases. They were running out of grapes, and soon expanded from their initial 62 acres of vineyards. Paul's business partner Roger was never satisfied with acquiring things. So they purchased another farm in the area. Not long after that, they heard that the open field on York Road across from where Paul was building his house was going to be for sale.

When Paul heard it was going to be sold for light industrial use, he said "Jesus! You're not going to put light industrial right across the street from my house!" He told Roger "I mean, we've gotta try to acquire that land!" Roger had a connection, and they did acquire it. They paid $4,000 an acre, and everyone said he'd been ripped off. Paul never wavered, and he was right. In later years, it was worth a lot more. His neighbour paid $40,000 per acre when he bought the adjacent land, ten times what Paul paid for his. The cost of land per acre was much much much lower than today. It wasn't like they had a lot of money, but as long as they were a little bit profitable, and on side with their bank, they were amenable to loaning them money for an asset. Paul and his partners had enough money to put into a deal and the bank would backstop them for the rest.

Making the wine sales, however, was a time consuming and often humbling endeavour with its own ups and downs.

Madame Bosc did her part for sales. She poured samples and charmed customers one at a time at a makeshift tasting table roadside at the winery. Many evenings after teaching school all day she'd pack up her car with cases of wine and drive to wine tasting events in Toronto. Debi Pratt was doing the same thing for Inniskillin. She also worked full time as a teacher. The two women would see each other across the aisle at the wine event as they set up and tore down their tasting supplies. They'd give each other a nod and a wave, acknowledging their mutual exhaustion—and passion—to help their wineries succeed.

The LCBO was a total monopoly. The first hurdle was to get your wine listed.

Paul would present his wines to the brand manager at the LCBO office. Once a brand was accepted by the LCBO, the stores had to put it on the shelves. It was called a forced listing. It wouldn't be for all LCBO stores, but for the size of his operation, Paul would be delighted if he got it for 200 stores, although 100 to 150 stores would be more typical. Even then, there was no guarantee that those 100 or 150 stores would put his wine on their shelves. The LCBO mandated it, but didn't enforce it. He was welcome to approach individual stores and try to persuade them to listen, so that's exactly what he did.

Every two months, Paul would be on the road visiting LCBO stores, checking to see if they were stocking his wine, and reminding them if they weren't. He would leave early in the morning, and be gone for days, but once he was gone he didn't have to worry, Andrée would take care of everything at home, and the business too. They worked hand in glove in a tight partnership from the beginning.

Paul would hit every single LCBO store between Ottawa and Niagara-on-the-Lake. Trenton, Belleville, Kingston, Tweed, and more. He would arrive at each store, no appointment, and ask to see the store manager. If the manager wasn't there, he'd ask for the assistant manager. Some of them were very, very rude. At one store, the manager came out and he was scowling. He must have been seven feet tall! He literally looked down on Paul, and growled derisively, "What the heck do you want!" Paul gathered himself up, all 5'7" of him, and said, "Well, I have your store on my list, for my wine to be listed, so I would really appreciate it if you stocked some of my wine here, because that's what most stores do." The manager seemed a little surprised he had failed to intimidate Paul. He paused, a bit flummoxed. Then he cracked a smile, and they had a good chat after all.

Paul had so many stores to visit, his stops would be fast. No small talk. He'd introduce himself, and tell them what he had listed that he'd like to see in the store. Ten minutes, in and out. Unless the manager liked Paul, and had heard of him and his wines. Then there would be a conversation. Paul wrote a brief report for each visit. It was just three or four lines, done in four or five minutes. Then he was done and on to the next store.

Paul Jr.'s summer job went from being a vineyard worker in high school to a salesman in university. When he walked into an LCBO store, he often encountered some bad attitudes. Either through apathy or incompetence, they typically hadn't read the full circular sent to every single store with all the listed wines. It could be 30 pages in before you would see the listing for Château des Charmes barrel fermented Chardonnay, brand number 81653. If the guy had been distracted or never read that far, then no one placed the order. After a while, Paul Jr. realized that most of the time in fact he wasn't proactively selling to an individual LCBO store, he was policing it. In a perfect world, he'd go back in a week to check, but that wasn't always possible.

Paul Sr. also approached other businesses and restaurants to get more exposure and sales for his wines.

One was Air Canada. As it was so often, this business arrangement flowed from a personal spark when Paul met with the person in charge. In this case, Paul went to see the right person at Air Canada, and they had lunch. They immediately hit it off. Paul was wearing a beautiful tailored jacket, and the guy from Air Canada really liked it. Simple things that create a connection can make a big difference, for better or for worse. In this case it was for the better. At first, Paul sold the airline a few cases of small bottles, and then ended up selling 30,000 cases over a few years. But then Paul discovered how personal connections could cut two ways.

The person Paul had dealt with originally moved on. The new person already had a partnership with some other people in the food and wine industry. There was no chemistry there to help cement a new relationship. When Paul told him he was going to have to buy some wine from other suppliers to keep making the same blend, because he didn't have enough supply of his own, the new guy made that an excuse to kick Paul out. He made a contract with his own associates to buy French wine for the airline. It was too bad, but it had been good while it lasted. A lot of people had been exposed to Château des Charmes, and would comment to him they'd had his wine on Air Canada. Paul had his ups and downs, but sales kept growing overall.

Restaurants were another potential source of sales. The way it worked, first you had to convince the restaurant to buy your wine, and then the sale still had to go through the LCBO.

Paul didn't call on too many restaurants. He focused on some large restaurants, like the CN Tower. He talked to the manager there. He was a German fellow, who had heard of Paul and his wines. He liked Paul right from the start, and it was his decision to make. "Okay, I'll put your wines in," he told Paul. "How much do you want to order?" asked Paul. "Oh, 1,000 cases of white, and 1,000 cases of red," he said. Paul caught his breath and smiled. "Of course," he said, beaming inside. That was a good sale.

It was an uphill struggle, but the wines spoke for themselves. They started to win over more and more restaurants as well as consumers.

Paul had been actively increasing Paul Jr.'s role and responsibilities ever since he'd helped out in the vineyards as a high school student. The plan was for Paul Jr. to be the sales and business leader. His gregarious personality and personal charm made him a perfect match for that arm of the business. Paul was quietly confident his son would make a career at the winery, and eventually lead the company. Paul Jr. himself wasn't yet certain that his future lay there. He was thinking about going to law school after his undergraduate studies.

When Paul Jr. was at the University of Toronto, other students may have worked for the summers at fast food restaurants or for house painting companies, but not him. He was an ambassador for Château des Charmes wines, doing his best to sell them to Toronto restaurants. Paul had no formal sales training, but he'd been a very, very good public speaker and debater in high school. He made the provincial finals in grade 11, competing against kids from the top private schools in Toronto. They were in grade 12 and grade 13. Public speaking and debating taught him to listen, to make eye contact, and be persuasive. Perhaps most importantly, it taught him to think on his feet. These were skills he would need in his early sales forays.

The toughest thing in those early years for Paul Jr. was having to make excuses for London Wines and Brights Wines, which were terrible. They had created a bad reputation for Ontario wines. The resistance and hostility could be palpable. You had to have a thick skin and a bucket of charm. Paul Jr. would somehow finagle a meeting with the food and beverage director of a hotel. He'd say, "I'm here to interest you in a quality Canadian wine." The reaction was instant. "Stop right there, don't you know what those are? Those are mutually exclusive terms, quality and Canadian wine. You guys don't produce Chardonnays and Rieslings down there in Niagara, you make Baby Duck and Moody Blue and Hochtaler!" The list went on. But Paul Jr. knew that a cornerstone of sales is that you have to be ready to overcome objections. He was tongue tied the first couple of times he met with that resistance, but then he came up with a strategy and some clever responses. He'd say, "Baby Duck. Yeah, that's really, really popular. We don't drink it in my house. I know that's what a lot of people want to buy, but thank goodness, things are changing. That's what I'm here to talk about today. Imports are getting more and more popular. What are imports made of? They're made of Chardonnay and Riesling and Pinot Noir and grapes like that. People want to drink either European wines, or wines with a European taste profile, from places like South Africa. We're now producing wines in the European style, in the European tradition," he would explain. Then Paul Jr. would leverage the family connection. He would say "I'm a kid, you know, I'm just a university student, but here's what I know. My dad is the most highly educated person in Canada when it comes to wine. He is a graduate of the University of Burgundy in Dijon, France. On top of that, he's a fifth generation French wine grower. And what this French guy has done is he's come to Canada and he has brought his French expertise and technology. We were the first to import 100% French oak barrels," he'd declare with pride. "Now, would you like to taste some of these wines?" he asked. And that would soften them up. Paul Jr. would get them to taste one of his Chardonnays and compare it to an imported Chardonnay. He figured he couldn't lose. Many people actually preferred the Château des Charmes wine. Even those who preferred the import a little bit, saw the value proposition. They would see that the quality was on a par with the French wine, and the cost was a bit lower. It was the only way to overcome the bad reputation Ontario wines had at the time.

Paul Jr. was trying to get his fathers' wines listed in high profile restaurants in Toronto. Winston's on Bay Street was the most famous restaurant in Canada, the place where power brokers dined. John Turner had his own table there, with his own phone on the table. The stakes were high when Paul Jr. got an appointment with the owner, John Arena. He was a slight Sicilian guy. Paul Jr. was only five nine, and still, he was looking down at him. Arena took the meeting, and they sat in his office. It was like the office of a bank president, almost regal. He did take the meeting, but then he beat Paul up. He challenged everything Paul Jr. said, very combatively. Eventually he said, "Look, you're wasting my time. You're not prepared, get out of here." And that was it. Paul Jr. was thrown out of Winston's. They didn't even get around to tasting the wine.

Paul Jr. trudged back to his little apartment, shoulders slumped and head down. He crawled into his bed, defeated. It was only the middle of the day, but it was over for him. Then his phone rang. It was his dad. He just had a hunch and called to see what Paul Jr. was up to. "Why are you at home, why are you not out selling?" Paul asked his son. "Well, I was out, but I went to Winston's and John Arena threw me out." Paul Jr. was crying. His dad wouldn't stand for it. "Why are you crying? Why didn't you just go to the restaurant next door? You know, knock on the door! Then if that guy throws you out, go to the next door after that, don't go home!" Paul exclaimed. "You better get out there tomorrow. Tomorrow morning. Get it together. And I'm not going to pay you for today. You didn't work so you're not going to get paid." Paul Jr. was crushed. About a week or so went by. He was thinking about that John Arena episode constantly. He didn't want to disappoint his dad. He didn't want him to think he was a loser. It wasn't as if he was striking out every time, he was making progress. He may have thought that he was better than he actually was, and John Arena reminded him that he still had a lot to learn. Almost in fear, Paul Jr. picked up the phone and called Arena back. He got him on the line and said, "you know, Mr. Arena, I've been thinking about our meeting, and I don't think you were fair with me. You didn't really give me a chance. But mostly you didn't give me a chance to have you taste the wines. You made some very good points, but your objections would have been addressed by tasting the wines. These are not Baby Duck. They're classic French varietals like Chardonnay and Riesling and Pinot Noir, produced by a fifth generation French winemaker from his own vineyard. My father makes wines completely in the French tradition. Our barrels are 100% French oak." Arena listened, and said, "Okay, kid. All right. You come back and we'll taste the wines." The next meeting with John Arena went much better. They ended up with two or three listings on the wine menu at Winston's. It was a huge feather in Paul Jr.'s cap, especially after his initial reception.

It was a pivotal experience for Paul Jr. He could have thought, "I didn't go to the University of Toronto to become a salesman, and I'm still thinking about law school". He could have said to his dad "I think I'll try for law school, and find a different job for next summer." But he decided to try again. He went back at it the following summer.

Paul Jr. got a call from John Arena that next summer. Arena had the contract to operate the facilities at Ontario Place including the Trillium dining room. He had decided to hold an Ontario Wine Festival at Ontario Place, and he invited Château des Charmes to participate. His daughter's boyfriend worked for Arena at the Trillium restaurant there, so he asked Paul Jr. to deal directly with him. When Paul Jr. met him, he found out he was also a student at the University of Toronto. It was great for Paul Jr. to be dealing with someone his own age for a change. The two hit it off, and had a successful collaboration. Months later, Paul Jr. was invited to John Arena's New Year's Eve party, at his uptown home. It was the preeminent social event in Toronto, a very tough ticket to get! Paul Jr. went to the party. He was looking around at all of Winston's famous customers—politicians, actors, bank presidents. He thought to himself, "Wow, in less than a year and a half I've gone from being thrown out of

John Arena's office, to being a guest in his home!" It had taken persistence, and some moxie. It was a meaningful moment.

A trade mission to Los Angeles cemented Paul Jr.'s commitment to joining his fathers business. Paul was in his third year at the University of Toronto. His dad asked him to represent Château des Charmes as part of a trade delegation to Los Angeles to promote Ontario wines. It turned out to be a formative experience. On the first day he was at the trade show, a young woman approached him. She started chatting with him. "You're the youngest guy here," she commented. She was a college student too, so they had that in common. She asked "what are you going to do in the evenings, when the show was closed?" Paul said "I'll probably have dinner with the other Ontario delegates, and hang out with them." She countered, asking him, "Would you like me to show you around,?" Paul took no time to say yes. The next three or four days were incredible. Paul almost didn't recognize the girl he'd met at the trade show when he went to her house. She looked completely different. She had 80's big hair and tight leather pants. She was very sexy. And she seemed to know everyone. She introduced Paul as her new friend from Canada. He felt like he was being treated like a king. There they were, on the sunset strip, rubbing shoulders with rock stars and actors. Paul was having so much fun in Los Angeles he didn't want to go home when the trade show was over. So he stayed. There was a flight home every day at the same time, so Paul delayed his return by a few days. He stayed on to party a little longer. It didn't cost anything to change his ticket, so it didn't cause any problems. That trip was the moment in time he decided that was what he wanted to do. He loved wine, he loved to party, and he loved to travel. He realized that working for his dad's business could be a vehicle to enjoy all three.

Although Paul Jr. was set on his career at Château des Charmes, he had an opportunity when he graduated from U of T to go to Ottawa and work as an aide to Eugene Whelan, the Minister of Agriculture. It was too good an opportunity to turn down. His parents were very proud of him. Paul Jr. would show them pictures of himself with Prime Minister Pierre Trudeau, and his dad was a big fan of Minister Whelan. At the time, though, Trudeau had become extremely unpopular in Western Canada, because of the National Energy Program. Whelan was really the only federal cabinet minister who could venture to Western Canada and not have tomatoes thrown at him. That great big Stetson hat he wore seemed to strike a better note west of Ontario, even though, in reality, he was from Amherstburg, Ontario. Whelan was travelling to make speeches all over the country, and Paul Jr. was travelling with him on government jets. The first time Paul Jr. flew out of Ottawa to points West, he was quite impressed. The seats were huge, like first class. There were ten or twelve seats. They each had built-in phones! That was like science fiction in the mid-80's. The steward pointed out that when they went from one airspace to another, they could make calls within that area. You couldn't make a national call but when you entered an airspace covered by the signal you could make a call within that area. He said to Paul Jr., "Hey, didn't you tell me you were from Niagara?" Paul Jr. said, "yeah, Niagara Falls actually." And the steward said, "Well, you know, we're flying above Toronto, and so we can call anywhere in southern Ontario. Why don't you call your parents?" Paul Jr. called them. His mom came on the phone first then his dad. Paul Jr. played a bit of a trick on them. He started a regular conversation, sort of shooting the breeze a little bit. Then his dad noticed a lot of background noise. "What, are you in a phone booth or in a windstorm or something?" Paul asked his son. "No, Dad, actually I'm on a government jet. With Minister Whelan. He'd like to say hi," Paul Jr. said. Mr. Whelan got on the line for 30 seconds or so. Whelan told Paul, "Hey, am I ever glad you let your boy come and join my team." Paul got back on the line and he said to Paul Jr., "Oh, you've got to talk to your mother!" Paul Jr. could hear the excitement and pride in his dad's voice. It was a very big deal for him. It had only been 21 years since he had to flee Algeria, and here was his son, on a government plane with the Minister of Agriculture. It was a big moment.

When that post ended, Paul was back at the winery full time. His dad could be hard on him, like that day he was thrown out of Winston's. He was not the type of guy to pat him on the head and tell him he was doing a good job. Feedback was more about where there was room for improvement. Paul wasn't afraid of humbling his son. But Paul Jr. knew his dad was hardest on himself. If he was tough with him, it was because he loved him and he wanted him to succeed. He thought it was like that Johnny Cash song, A Boy Named Sue. His dad thought he had to toughen him up. He learned to be very well prepared and have all of his ducks in a row when he met with his dad with a business proposal. He knew his dad had a lot going on, and got impatient easily.

It took a long time, but slowly and surely Paul Jr. built up his dad's trust. There were occasional setbacks. When he screwed up he'd hear about it. Paul Sr. had very high expectations. But a lot of good things happened. Paul Jr. had a great relationship with Paul's business partner, Roger, who really believed in him. That was very important to his dad. Roger would routinely show confidence in Paul Jr., and hand him more files to handle. Eventually, Paul said to his son, "Oh, we've got a meeting at the bank. Why don't you come along? It's got nothing to do with sales and marketing, but you never know, the banker might ask 'How's business', and you're best positioned to answer those questions." Paul Jr. did go to that bank meeting, and after that there was never a bank meeting he didn't go to. It was a gradual process, but Paul Jr. grew steadily into the role, and he pulled off some big wins in the years that followed.

The Tail that Wagged the Dog

As Paul Jr. had been experiencing first hand, selling Ontario wine was no easy task. The reputation of Ontario wines in the late 80s was dreadful. The negative reputation had been earned by poor quality wines. That was one major hurdle. The second came with the free trade agreement that took effect in 1988. It stripped away all the protections for Canadian wine. Most predicted the Canadian wine industry would simply collapse under the avalanche of cheap imported wine.

There were just over a dozen wineries operating in Ontario in the late 80's, some large, some small. There were six so-called "big boys"; Barnes, Brights, Château-Gai, Jordan, London, and Andrés. They made high volume wines with Labrusca varieties and hybrids, typically blended with international wines. International blends accounted for 80% of Ontario wine sales at that time.

There were nine smaller wineries. They included Inniskillin, Château des Charmes, Newark, Reif Estate, Vineland Estates, Konzelmann Estates, Stoney Ridge, Cave Spring Cellars, and Henry of Pelham. They made wine from exclusively locally grown grapes, most of them vinifera varieties. Together they only represented a fraction of the market but they were fierce in their determination to pull the industry into a sustainable future.

That band of passionate pioneers not only persisted in growing vinifera grapes, they simply weren't willing to accept defeat in the face of free trade. They reasoned that their industry needed a new model, to shift away from making boatloads of plonk and selling it cheaply. Instead, the future would be in making smaller quantities of quality wine, and selling it for what it was worth. They were too naive to listen to prevailing opinion predicting disaster. They soldiered on.

Donald Ziraldo of Inniskillin realized that they needed an appellation system, akin to those in other wine regions. It would set quality standards, and communicate those standards to consumers. If they could label their wines under an appellation system, it would differentiate them from other Canadian wines of lower quality and those with offshore blends. Donald led the charge, and Paul Bosc Sr. became the standard bearer for the highest levels of quality. Both men were very familiar with the European systems for exactly that, such as the AOC in France (Appellation d'Origine Contrôlée), and the DOC (Controlled Denomination of Origin) system in Italy. The goal was to raise the bar for the Canadian industry, to create elevated standards in order to survive and compete against the tsunami of imported wine coming in with the advent of free trade.

Ziraldo soon rallied a willing team of like minded visionaries. Paul Bosc needed no convincing. Len Pennachetti of Cave Spring volunteered, and soon spent all his waking hours consumed with the task of establishing what would become known as the VQA, short for the Vintners Quality Alliance. Paul Speck at Henry of Pelham was all in. He was excited about the prospects. He thought, "Well, you know, these guys know what they're doing, we should be able to do something here." He was very enthusiastic. His girlfriend (and later wife) Melissa dubbed Len as Paul's work husband during that time because they were spending so much time working together, at night and on the weekends. Allan Schmidt of Vineland Estates was a founding committee member. Donna Lailey was there as a grower. She was the lone woman. Karl Kaiser was there representing Inniskillin. Klaus Reif and Herbert Konzelmann were also key contributors too, bringing their own passion for wine and their deep family roots from the wine industry in Germany.

This small cadre of enthusiasts started meeting regularly. They would attend regular meetings of the Ontario Wine Council, along with the big commercial producers. It was the only industry group back then, and focused on promotion, marketing, and lobbying the LCBO. After the Wine Council meetings, the small winery folks would split off on their own to meet about the VQA. The bigger players were aware of what the upstarts were doing, but they weren't interested. They didn't take the notion seriously. They were like, "Hey kids have fun. You can borrow the boardroom for your meetings. You want free coffee? Here you go." They had zero interest in it. It wasn't their game.

The leaders from the small wineries drank a lot of coffee around that table, and spent a lot of time debating. They weren't trying to re-invent the wheel, just to emulate existing appellation systems. They were referencing the AOC and DOC from Europe, as well as the relatively more recent American standards. Ziraldo was the visionary, Paul Sr. was the elder statesman, and together they were a band of entrepreneurial dreamers.

The leadership at the table quickly reached a consensus on the need for elevated standards in order to survive. The debates and arguments were all about the details, and exactly how high that standard should be. The tension was between the practicality of wine makers having flexibility on one hand, while maintaining a high quality standard on the other. There was always heated debate in the room—a tug of war between the two ends of that spectrum. Paul was steadfastly uncompromising on the side of quality. He was the conscience of the group.

As an example of where they were starting from, they had to actually include language to strictly prohibit the addition of water to wine. The Europeans around the table were horrified to realize that was a common practise at the time in Ontario, because there were no rules or standards. It was known as stretching. In Europe, that would be considered fraud because it was against established regulations. In Ontario it was an everyday technique used to produce more wine cheaply. Then sugar would be added to get more alcohol. Much of what was made and sold was a confected product, not really wine at all. That's what they were up against. They knew they had to pivot from where the industry was to a future where they were making world class wine.

Len did the heavy lifting, taking meticulous handwritten notes and keeping records. Eventually the meetings yielded a documented set of rules, and they started getting some traction in the industry. It was a volunteer club to begin with, but no one could use VQA on their labels if they didn't comply with the newly documented standards.

Len credited Paul with the discipline that went into the standards. They may not have been rigorous enough in some ways, but they would not have been as rigorous as they were if Paul hadn't been in the room. He was a leader who kept them honest, never wavering when it came down to a question of whether they should take the easy path. He was always vigilant about not compromising quality and that really drove the early history of the VQA. They created a category that allowed them to continue to compete, and it was built on quality. That's why the Q is in the VQA. Ziraldo came up with the name at the beginning, and Paul Sr. defended quality at every turn.

The first vintage that the new VQA standards applied to was 1988. The first wines that met the standards and were qualified to put "VQA" on their labels had been bottled much earlier. Since it was too late to incorporate "VQA" on the bottles that were already labeled, they had VQA stickers printed. Wineries could put the stickers on the wines that qualified.

Right around that time, Paul Speck was very excited that one of the top restaurants in Toronto, Scaramouche, had a Henry of Pelham Chardonnay on their wine list. He and his wife Melissa went there for dinner. Paul talked to the chef, and said, "We're here for dinner, but first, do you mind if I go in the back?" Paul went into the wine storage area, and he opened up all the boxes from Henry of Pelham. He pulled the bottles out, and slapped VQA stickers on each one. He went back to their table, and he and Melissa had dinner. Later he called a friend and said, "God, we just spent $100 on dinner!" It might as well have been a million dollars. The food was good, and they had a bottle of their own Chardonnay, which cost a lot more than they thought it should.

Of course there was no VQA section at the LCBO in those days, so their wines got shelved with Baby Duck and everything else. They lobbied the LCBO. It wasn't easy, but they did get a VQA space, and started to get some promotion. That was a game changer. But it was still an uphill battle for the wine to be recognized as a higher quality worthy of a higher price. Paul Speck wanted to price one of his Henry of Pelham wines at $8.95 a bottle. The buyer at the LCBO told him, "There's no way, no one's going to buy it at that price! Ontario wine for $8.95? No way!" The buyer countered with $7.45. Paul pushed back with $7.95, and that's where it ended up. It was a very different world.

Change was afoot with the advent of the VQA, but the tide was also turning in the vineyards. The federal and provincial governments launched something called the "Grape and Wine Adjustment Program", to provide some aid to grape growers in the face of free trade. It quickly became known by the more colloquial name, the "Pullout Program." Growers were compensated for pulling out vines not suitable for quality winemaking, mostly labrusca varieties as well as some hybrids. While slow to take off at the start, vines were eventually removed from more than 8,000 acres, mostly between 1989 and 1991. Growers were paid $1,100 per acre. This literally cleared the way for the broader transformation to vinifera grapevines, finally falling into step with the ambitious dreams of the early innovators. In 1980, there were 800 tons of vinifera harvested. By 1990, that number increased to 4,000 tons, and ten years after that, the volume surged to more than 20,000 tons. The early innovators had been proved right, but the irony here was that the pioneers who took the gamble to plant vinifera early on got nothing from this program. Instead it rewarded those growers who stuck with their labrusca vines until the writing was on the wall. There was, however, another assistance program called the Ontario Winery Assistance Program to support expansion and upgrading of wineries to help make them more competitive. Many of the early wineries did benefit from that program. It helped them buy new equipment, invest in sales and marketing, or build new facilities.

In 1990, Peter Gamble was hired as the founding Executive Director of the VQA. Peter had been the winemaker at Hillebrand, and he was an internationally recognized wine taster and writer. The regulations were up and running but there was a lot of follow up work to do, especially on matters that had been contentious, such as the use of some lesser French hybrid grapes within the VQA designation. Paul went to all the meetings. He'd often lay in wait until there was a critical point in making a decision on whether they were going to accept a looser standard. Whatever that looser standard might have been, Paul would stand up and with real passion, often very loudly and always laced with expletives, blast the room. "Why would we do this? This is ridiculous, we can't do this!" Once he'd finished going on for a few minutes, he'd sit down. Nobody else would dare stand up again. They'd take the vote and very often, Paul would carry the room and protect the higher standard. Peter was almost infallibly on side with Paul, as were some of the others who were there, but nobody was as forceful or as vocal about it. That process went on for several years. By then the bigger players were at the table too, having purchased or merged with some of the key wineries that were making VQA wine, including Hillebrand and Inniskillin.

Over those years, there was a lot of consolidation going on with the larger entities. Brights bought Jordan, Château-Gai bought Barnes, and then a management buyout of Château-Gai led by Allan Jackson and Don Triggs created Cartier Wines, which in turn merged with Inniskillin. The Jackson-Triggs group bought Brights and London to form Vincor. Andrès bought Hillebrand (formerly Newark). That meant there were just two commercial players, Vincor and Andrés, and they became much bigger. Their acquisitions included wineries that were producing wine from vinifera grapes, such as Inniskillin and Hillebrand. That fact, plus the realization that consumers were beginning to embrace the VQA quality wines, brought the big players to the VQA table as it continued to develop. They were late to the party. They tried to hang on to as much flexibility as they could, but they realized they'd have to join in if they wanted to market their own wines with the VQA endorsement.

The process culminated in The Vintners Quality Act in 1999, shifting the voluntary industry program to government regulation. It provided for independent oversight, strengthened enforcement, and it built trust with consumers and trading partners. Canada's preeminent wine expert Tony Aspler wrote that it was "the single most important piece of legislation to save the industry from extinction. The small players had become the engine that propelled Ontario wines, dragging the large commercial players reluctantly along in their combined wake." (*Wine Atlas of Canada*)

While International Domestic Blends, which only had to use 25% Ontario wine with 75% imported, would continue to dominate wine sales, the number of wineries making VQA wines made with 100% Ontario grapes showed growth. From that first cohort of nine wineries that set out to create the VQA in 1988, membership grew to 51 members in 2000; and 192 members by 2024. Multiple international awards soon recognized the quality of the wines, and consumers followed suit. Sales of VQA wines went from $144 million in 2001 to $403 million in 2024. Several of the key leaders involved in setting up the VQA were eventually recognized with the Order of Canada for their contributions to the industry, including Len Pennachetti, Donald Ziraldo, and Paul Bosc Sr.

Paul Bosc with cousin Pierrette Fischer, 1937 (Credit: Armand Bosc)

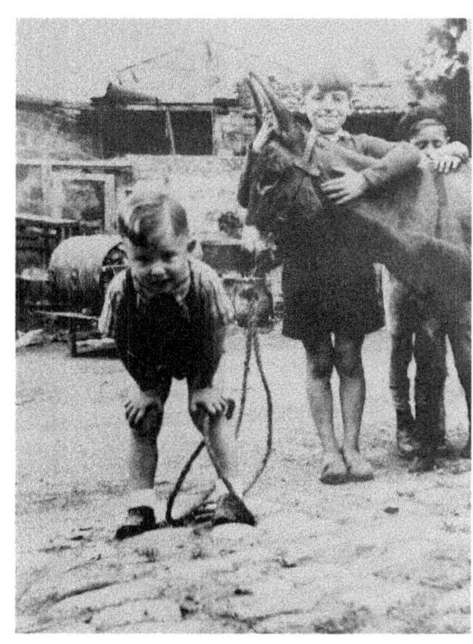

Paul (standing, centre) with his beloved donkey Toki, in Algeria

Carefree at the beach with friends in Algeria

Paul Sr., a young man in Paris

Paul (left) with army comrades during his service in France

Wedding picture, Paul & Andrée, 1958

With his mother, Suzanne in Algeria

Label from wine made at the co-op in Marengo, Algeria where Paul worked

Paul with Château-Gai sparkling wines

Bosc Family at their home in Niagara Falls during the Château Gai years

On sunny Saturdays, Madame moved tastings roadside to enjoy the nice weather just outside the warehouse door. Her checkered tablecloth added a dash of style, with pallets and farm equipment in the background

Original bottling line in the cinderblock building on Creek Road, assembled with various second-hand parts,1979

Paul Sr. grafting vines for his own vineyards on Creek Road in March 1979. By the mid-80s, he was grafting 100,000 vines per year as a nursery business, to support the winery during its start-up phase.

Doing chores in the quonset hut on Creek Road in 1978, with his original—used—press. It worked until 1994, when the operation moved to the Château on York Road.

Paul Sr. as Grape King, 1988. It was a great honour

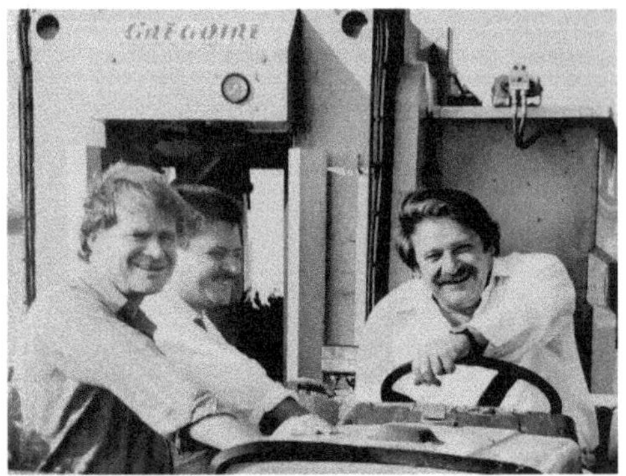

On new harvester, with Paul Jr. No more second-hand equipment, 1990

Paul Sr., Paul Jr., and Stephan with awards from Cuvée, 1992

The imposing Château, opened in 1995

Paul Bosc receiving Order of Canada pin from Governor General Michaëlle Jean

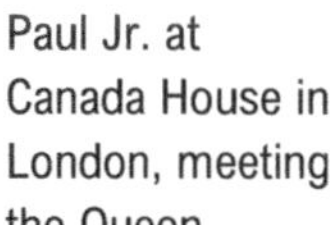

Paul Jr. at Canada House in London, meeting the Queen

Paul Jr. with Pierre Trudeau

Paul Sr. (right) with his trainer Richard Biele behind the Château

Father & son in the vineyard

Paul Jr., his wife Michèle, and a young Alex in the vineyard

Family home in Niagara-on-the-Lake

Paul Sr., Madame, Paul Jr., Michèle

In the vineyard

Paul Sr. & winemaker Amélie Boury in the vineyard

Paul Sr. with Amélie at a wine trade show in France, November 2016

Paul Sr. with Amélie in March 2018

Amélie & Cassandra harvesting in 2020

Paul Sr. having a beer with his workers at a nearby farm

Paul Jr. with Marco Piccoli, the new CEO at Château des Charmes, on the day the sale was announced, June 2024

Paul Sr. on his last trip to France

Amélie starts the 2024 harvest, picking Chardonnay grapes for sparkling wine

2024 harvest at the Château, the first harvest after Paul Sr.'s death

Part Three

Growing Success

Memorable Milestones and Building Blocks

During those same years that the VQA was being developed and beyond, work at the Paul Bosc winery never let up. A series of memorable moments unfolded, pinnacles of success that marked the progress of Château des Charmes. Their wines won prominence at competitions at home and abroad. They were chosen to be served at prestigious events with world leaders; and Paul was personally highly honoured for his contributions. All of that, plus the opening of the grand bricks and mortar Château. It was a forerunner of future wineries in Niagara designed for function as well as emerging wine tourism.

Over time, Paul became more confident. He started entering his wines in international wine competitions like VinExpo in France or the International Wine and Spirits competition in London, England. His 1991 vintage Paul Bosc Estate Vineyard Chardonnay won a gold medal at VinExpo in 1993. It was the first Canadian table wine to win there. Two years later, two Bordeaux style red wines from the same vineyard won gold medals. The judging panels were French, and the competition was in the heart of Bordeaux, so those wins were truly remarkable.

Eventually, he and Paul Jr. decided to take their act further and further out on the road. They won over an importer in Japan who stayed with them for 30 years. They established a lasting relationship with Disney World in Florida. They even sold their wine to Costco in the southwest of the U.S. and in California. They secured an importer in Bermuda for more than 20 years. Maybe the cherry on top of it all was a deal with an importer in France of all places. It's not a big sale every year, maybe two thousand bottles of wine, but that's Niagara wine being sold in France! Definitely a source of bragging rights.

That importer in France played a central role in one of Paul's favourite stories. He and Paul Jr. were at VinExpo in France. One of their buyers from Niagara was there too. His name was Louis. He owned Aielli Restaurant in Port Credit. Louis had never been to Paris, so they offered to show him around for a night or two. Before they chose where to go, Paul Jr. asked his importer a question. "If we go out on the town with one of our customers from back home, where are the restaurants that have our wine? So we can thank the restaurateur for his business, and maybe show off our presence a little." The importer said "Sure, here are a few restaurants you can go to, they have your wine on their lists." They took Louis to one of those restaurants for dinner. Lo and behold, there were Château des Charmes wines on the menu! They enjoyed a bottle of Pinot Noir together. Louis was very impressed. Of course the not so subtle message to him was that these wines weren't just good enough for his restaurant in Mississauga, they were good enough for restaurants in Paris, France! It may have been a bit of a set up, but it did the trick. Louis told that story hundreds of times after that. That's how they turned people into evangelists, one by one.

Ottawa — '79 into '80's

Early wins paved the way for bigger triumphs to come. Not only was Paul a pioneer in the vineyards, he and his son were leading the way in creating acceptance and appreciation of Ontario wines. One of the friendlier environments in the beginning was Ottawa. It's much smaller than Toronto, and Ontario wines made an early impact there. Of course Ottawa is the nation's capital. Much is driven by politicians and the political culture there. One of the turning points was when Joe Clark was Prime Minister. As an economic nationalist, he liked to buy Canadian. He was also a fan of Niagara wines. Clark was the first high profile politician with that attitude. All of a sudden the LCBO was getting orders from 24 Sussex or from External Affairs, for 20 cases of Château des Charmes Chardonnay, and 20 cases of Inniskillin Marechal Foch. The LCBO had to scramble to buy enough, and that gained attention. Also, the wines started being served at very high profile events. Even after Clark was no longer Prime Minister, when he was at the official residence at Stornaway as Opposition Leader, he started an annual event there to taste Canadian wines. Paul Jr. was still in university at the time, and to him that first event looked like a scene out of The Great Gatsby. Stornoway is a 100 year old mansion, and there was a tent set up, with people in summer attire milling about. The men were in white suits, the women in stylish cocktail dresses. A live quartet played jazz in the background, and waiters in white shirts and black ties circulated with elegant hors d'oeuvres and glasses of wine. Clark wanted the wines to be positioned as classy, and premium. The event was catered by his personal chef. Invitations went out to prominent people, ambassadors, senior mandarins in the federal government, political opponents even. It was at that event where Paul Jr. met Peter Ward, for the first time, who became the wine writer for the *Ottawa Citizen.* Minds were changed at that event. People discovered they liked Ontario wines. Clark kept it going for several years. Then, when the Château Laurier was hosting a big federal government event, a state dinner or something like that, they would order Canadian wine. Then Prime Minister Trudeau started coming around too, and Château des Charmes began supplying his annual Christmas party and summer party. At events like those there were maybe 40 cases being served, and hundreds of people attending. Then the Governor General started coming around, and there were significant orders coming from Rideau Hall. That's when it started to steamroll. So whether it was Paul Sr. or Paul Jr., they had all kinds of reasons to hit the road and go all the way up to Ottawa, to do a tasting, or a dinner.

Once they were there, they always got on local radio or TV programs. Paul had a big profile, and people would see his face, and remember him from the commercial back from his days at Château-Gai. Ottawa was fertile ground for winning new fans for their wine. Those early wins eventually translated to much bigger ones to come.

Shamrock Summit, March 1985

Many Canadians recall the Shamrock Summit held in March 1985. Prime Minister Brian Mulroney hosted U.S. President Ronald Reagan at meetings followed by a gala event in Quebec City. The televised scene of the two leaders and their wives singing "When Irish Eyes are Smiling" as they joined hands became an enduring symbol of the camaraderie between Mulroney and Reagan.

For Paul, that summit was also a major milestone. The government chose Château des Charmes wine to be served at the summit. It was a very big deal.

Their estate bottled Pinot Noir, vintage 1982, was served. It was a very small production, only 500 cases were made. Fifty cases went to that event. Paul liked to tell that story over the years. Sometimes he would challenge a French wine producer, saying, "you know what's nice about a small wine country like Canada? Here in your native France, there are thousands and thousands and thousands of wine producers. Have your wines ever been served at state events?

Did Francois Mitterrand ever call you to serve your wine when he was President? Our prime minister called on us to serve our wine at an important event. Then in 1991 my wife and I were invited by Prime Minister Mulroney and his wife to a dinner party at 24 Sussex, their official residence. Of course they had our wines there too. In France, you don't get those opportunities. Here, being a bigger fish in a smaller pond gets us into places that others don't."

There were many other honours over the years, and Paul was always happy about them, but these early moments were the most memorable bright spots on a journey that included so much hard work and so many obstacles.

In the Vineyards

Even as accolades and wins mounted, challenges never ceased. Paul Sr. had a stable crew of skilled workers, the fans kept his vines unharmed in severe cold, and growing vinifera had become the established norm. But then a new threat emerged.

Paul was always adamant about waiting for the precise moment when the grapes were perfectly ripe for optimal harvesting. When the moment came, Paul knew he had to move fast. So for a few years, he had Mattias Oppenlaender harvesting for him, with a French mechanical harvester. Paul wanted to try it out before making the investment himself. He would say to Oppenlaender, "I know my Chardonnay will be ready on Wednesday and Thursday, and they're calling for rain on Friday. So don't book anyone else. You're going to be here." Sometimes they would actually pick for 24 hours if they had to. And Paul would always be there.

When they picked late at night, he would come out, and sit in the pickup truck with Oppenlaender, and talk about his experiments and experiences. He was too busy for conversation most of the time, but Oppenlaender loved hearing his stories on those late nights, while the harvester's headlights bobbed through the vineyard in the dark of the night.

The growing season in 2001 was picture perfect. Paul had been carefully nurturing his chardonnay vines on his estate property on York Road. As always, he was very picky about choosing the optimal ripeness for harvest. Finally, the grapes were pristine, and perfectly ripe. Oppenlaender and his crew were in the vineyard. They were just a couple of hours into the harvest. It was a beautiful sunny day. Paul came out to see how it was going. Oppenlaender had bad news.

He had discovered ladybugs.

Oppenlaender had never seen Paul so mad. His frustration boiled over, and his normal composure broke down. Ladybugs could be a disaster, and the harvest had been looking so perfect. The whole season could be a loss if they couldn't manage to get rid of the ladybugs and still harvest before the grapes got overripe. It was a race against time. Ladybugs would contaminate the wine, and create what is known as ladybug taint. It's a horrible flaw that destroys the quality of the wine.

Paul knew what he had to do. He asked Oppenlaender to spray for the ladybugs, then they'd have to wait at least two days before trying to harvest again. They'd just have to cross their fingers that the grapes wouldn't get overripe and the weather would stay dry. The day they would be harvesting, Paul had a critical meeting with his bank, so he couldn't be there as the harvest started. It nearly killed him to miss it. The minute his meeting was over, he dashed straight to the vineyard, in his pinstripe suit and gold cufflinks. He had to see how it was going. There was no time to change his shoes! The good news was that the ladybugs were gone and the weather had been co-operative. The harvest was saved. One more potential catastrophe dodged.

Paul was not only passionate about his own operations. He was ready, willing, and able to help others. He was a very caring person. One story in particular stands out.

Late one Saturday evening, Oppenlaender's crew was harvesting in one of Paul's fields, when Oppenlaender got a call. "We hit a hole or something and the harvester flipped over," his guy told him. Harvesters are huge lumbering machines. It would be a big deal to get it set right again. Oppenlaender called Paul. He said, "Don't worry, I'll get it out. We'll get it done." Another person might have walked away and left it as Oppenlaender's problem to deal with, but not Paul. He was on it.

Paul had made connections with crane operators in the area when he was installing his fans. He made a call to one of them, to come and help get the mammoth harvester upright. Before they knew it, this guy showed up. He said, "Oh man, I was at home on a Saturday night watching the hockey game with my wife when Paul called. But here I am!" Paul was watching, and he asked the crane operator to do his best to limit the damage to the vines. Finally the big machine was back on its feet, and the damage had been limited. It was a success, but it had been a long and stressful night for the handful of men working that night. Paul said, "Come on, there was a wedding at the Château tonight, but it's over now. Let's all go there now and have dinner."

The Long Road to Building the Château

A cinderblock building that stood on Four Mile Creek Road housed a small tasting area for Château des Charmes through the 1980's and into the mid-90's. It was easy to be overwhelmed there when a bus or two pulled in!! There were tables in the parking lot to do tastings for large groups, but if it rained or snowed, the entire bus would empty into the building, with everyone elbow to elbow. Madame, as she was known, was the ebullient host. Guests remembered their experiences with her for years afterwards. It would never occur to her to send people away, just because the boutique was so small. She would put on a show for her visitors. Madame would disappear into a back room and come back brandishing a bottle of wine. She'd say, conspiratorially, "Oh don't tell my husband I'm serving you this wine, it's very special! Don't tell him I'm opening this for you." It may have been mostly show business, but her guests loved it. They loved it.

Paul's plan was to build the Château on that same plot of land that fronted onto Four Mile Creek Road and Line 7. He thought it would take three to five years from when he started up the winery on that site in the late '70s. He knew he needed a new home for his production facilities, and also to welcome tourists to taste and buy his wines. The next one would not only have to be larger to accommodate, hopefully, the growing sales. It would also have to be a lot prettier than a plain square cinder block building. He had looked around and he could see where the future was, because even then, by the mid to late 70s in California, wine tourism was taking off. Robert Mondavi built his winery in 1966, and the place was packed with tourists by the 70's. Paul had Niagara Falls right next door, drawing 15 million visitors a year, and the town of Niagara-on-the-Lake was becoming popular. It was a nice little tourist spot, and the Shaw Festival was doing very, very well by then. So even though Paul's focus had always been on growing the best grapes and making the best wine he could, he also realized he'd have to allocate resources for something impressive to leverage the emerging tourism trade. He knew it would become an important aspect of future success.

Little did he know then, it would actually take, not three to five years, but 16 years to build his Château, and it would be in a completely different location.

The 1980's were very tough even on the large, established wine businesses in Niagara. For Paul, just starting out with a new business, the margin for error was non-existent. The challenges in the industry at large were even harder for him to weather, as a smaller operation. Château des Charmes was in survival mode during that decade. It was fighting for sales and developing its vineyards. It was not in a financial position to invest in building a Château.

One significant factor was the Free Trade Agreement. Talks began in the mid 80's, ironically kicked off at the very Shamrock Summit that featured Château des Charmes Pinot Noir. There was a lot of controversy over the whole agreement. The publicity campaign generated by the wine industry in an effort to defeat ratification of the agreement backfired. The public was not sympathetic. It viewed the industry as being afraid to compete. Sales of Ontario wines started to fall even before the Free Trade Agreement was implemented. When the increased markups on Canadian wine were slapped on as a result of the agreement, their market share dropped a whopping 20 points.

Paul did achieve many milestones during that decade. He was producing high quality wine, and making gains on the sales front. But it was tough going, and it didn't produce the financial results he'd need to build a Château. In one way, though, the delay turned out to be a blessing in disguise, because an opportunity arose for Paul to acquire a much better site for the future Château than his property on Four Mile Creek.

Paul and Andrée had purchased land on York Road to build their new home in 1982. Five years later, in 1987, the land right across the street became available, and Paul recognized what a perfect spot it was for the future Château. It was nestled right up against the Niagara Escarpment on St. David's Bench, a perfect site to grow and ripen fine Bordeaux grapes for red wine. It was close to the highway making it convenient for visitors to access it. And York Road had just been named the Wine Route.

From the day they purchased that land in 1987, they were driven to build the Château. It would be a few more years before it became a reality. Actually, eight more years. For all of their anticipation, very very few people knew there were plans afoot until one day there was a groundbreaking ceremony, and then a sign was erected, "Future Home of Château des Charmes." Paul didn't believe in talking about plans before they were real.

For many years Paul had thought about what his ideal Château would be like. He wanted state of the art production facilities, expansive and sophisticated spaces for tourists, and of course the visual impression of a grand Château set amongst vineyards planted right up to the edge of the towering escarpment. When the time came to give instructions to the architect, his vision was well formed.

For his production facilities, he specified the fermentation area would be on one side, with a huge underground cellar in the middle, and on the other side a warehouse and bottling room.

In terms of style, Paul loved old Canadian buildings, like the elegant Château Laurier Hotel in Ottawa, so he told the architect that was the style he wanted. He wanted his Château to echo the old railroad hotels that had been built along the rail lines as they expanded across the country, with their steep roofs, turrets, and copper-clad towers. He was adamant that everything would be symmetrical. "What you have on one side you've got to have on the other side. And no corners here and there where we waste space," he instructed them. His directions must have been very clear, because they hit it right with the first design, although the first drawings envisioned a bigger Château than what was ultimately built. The price was too high, so they had to revise the plan. When they came back with the smaller version, Paul was happy with it. And he built it. It had been16 years since the company started, but finally Paul was building his Château.

Of course, there was a grand fête to celebrate the grand opening. Paul Jr. organized the event. It took him months. When the day came, Paul was very excited. He and his partner Roger made speeches. There were various dignitaries there, including Andy Brandt, the chair of the LCBO. Premier Bob Rae couldn't be there, but he had come for a private visit a week earlier. 500 people gathered outside, in front of the Château for all the pomp and circumstance. Paul Jr. was the master of ceremonies. As the formalities drew to a close, the sun sank to the horizon and lights were doused so all was in darkness. It seemed everyone held their breath for a moment. Then the show began. There was music, and fireworks lit up the new Château like a Disney castle. The doors were thrown open, and everyone went inside, eager to see the beautiful interior. The front doors opened onto a gracious foyer with a spectacular chandelier and a curving staircase. There were various tasting rooms and a boutique. Food and wine stations were set up all over the Château. The food was prepared by the best chefs in Niagara, and the wine was the best Château des Charmes had to offer. The event garnered a lot of publicity, with coverage on national newscasts that night, and a live segment on Canada AM with Keith Morrison. It was a big deal, and not only for the Bosc family.

It was important because Canada and Ontario were in a serious recession at the time. The year the Château was built, there were only two building projects in the Niagara region with a value of $5 million or more, and the Château was one of them. The other one was a school. The economy was not looking good in Niagara, yet Paul had decided to throw caution to the wind, and go ahead despite the recession. His courage to take chances created opportunities not just for himself, but for his competitors and colleagues as well. One commentator called it a major turning point for the Ontario wine industry. He predicted that in the years to come as a result of this, wine making and wine tourism would become an economically important industry in the region of Niagara and in the province of Ontario. He was right. He made that prediction, and that's what happened.

Paul's belief in "If you build it, they will come," became an instant reality. From the day it opened, the Château was very busy. They were heady days. Château des Charmes had a real head start, a clear competitive advantage. It all centred on Paul's talent and expertise in growing grapes and making wine, and then building the Château created a state of the art production facility as well as a perfect location to grow the emerging agri-tourism trade. The other grand winery buildings that followed and now dot the region were still years away.

Madame Andrée was still teaching when the Château opened. She would go there after work. She'd park in the back, in the warehouse area where no one was supposed to park. But no one was going to be the one to tell her to move her car. Paul Jr. would be in his office on the second floor, and he'd know when she was there. He'd hear her footsteps clickety clack on the tile floors, tapping out a brisk staccato. She was always in a hurry, her energy was frenetic.

She was very happy when she retired from teaching, and took up her role at the Château full time. With her beloved white Bichon Frisé Michon tucked into her elbow, Madame would hold court with visitors. Many came expressly in the hope of seeing her. She was very socially outgoing, unlike Paul, who preferred the quiet of the vineyard. Madame was a storyteller extraordinaire. No one minded if there were embellishments, they just made the stories even more entertaining. Sparkling wine would flow, and she'd sit, in her trademark caftan and clogs, regaling guests with whatever tales were top of mind on a given day. Her heavy French accent and strong manner of speaking captivated her audiences, and her mannerisms were very emotive. She was larger than life.

Madame made such an impression on her guests, they just kept coming back. Some who came to the Château remembered Madame from her days pouring wine on Creek Road, at the original winery. They'd revel in their memories of those experiences, saying "In those days, we'd hang out with Madame all day, and then we would wash glasses with her and help clean up." It was a special relationship.

As if teaching, raising a family, and working at the winery were not enough, Madame's hands were never idle. She knitted and crocheted endless numbers of comforters and throws. She made more than 100 baby blankets, and she would give them to customers. Years later, a 30 year old man came to the winery and told Paul Jr. that he'd been coming to the Château since he was a baby. He said Madame had given his parents a baby blanket when he was born, and he still treasured it.

Not long after the Château opened, Paul Jr. hired Suzanne Janke as a Special Events Coordinator. Paul Sr. gave his stamp of approval, and then Suzanne met Madame. It wasn't easy for her at the beginning. Madame was very guarded. It was awkward being a new employee in a fairly senior role in a family enterprise that had been so close knit for so many years. Madame was the matriarch. She was firm and assertive, but underneath it, warm, like a grandmother, but you had to earn her trust. Nobody could come in and just crack the code, it took a while. She wanted to see that you were committed to her business and loyal. Suzanne demonstrated her dedication and work ethic, and eventually Madame embraced her and they became close friends. Suzanne herself was the recipient of one of Madame's baby blankets when her first child was born.

Weddings and private events became an important aspect of the business. Madame would often watch them happen. She just loved seeing everybody having so much joy at her property. Sometimes, as the events manager, Suzanne would be concerned that there'd be confusion. Madame wasn't an invited guest, per se, but she would be out there feeling like she was part of the party. But people just loved that the matriarch of the winery was there.

She'd be there till three in the morning, and then she'd be right back at it next thing in the morning, seven days a week. She would never say,"Oh, I'm taking today off." She never went on vacation. There were no days off.

Tastings continued, and there were more and more weddings at the Château. Couples were drawn to the romantic setting in the beautiful vineyard tucked in against the escarpment. Tourism was poised to grow, and it certainly did. At that time, the wine route may have attracted 200,000 people in a year. Thirty years later, that number had climbed enormously, to 2.4 million people. The economic impact grew as well. Tourism related spending added up to $2.4 billion dollars a year. It was like throwing a pebble into the pond and seeing it ripple out, getting wider and wider. Opening the Château provided momentum for many years to come, both for winemaking and visitor experiences.

Time for a Twin Passion

Paul loved animals, period. But horses in particular held a special place in his heart.

Paul learned to ride as a youngster in Algeria. When he was six years old, his family had a donkey named Toki. Paul loved that donkey. He taught himself how to ride it.

Sometimes Toki would throw Paul off his back. Paul would get up and brush himself off, and get right back on. Eventually Toki accepted Paul riding him, and they were inseparable. One day when Paul came home from school, he had a heartbreaking surprise. He discovered that his mother had sold Toki. Paul considered Toki a pet and a member of the family, but to his parents he was just a beast of burden. When someone came along and offered a few francs for him it was just a good price for an old donkey. Paul was devastated. Toki had ignited Paul's lifelong passion for horses, and he never forgot that donkey.

Later, Paul rode the horses on his grandparents farm, and learned how to care for them. The hours he spent at the barn flew by. He was happiest when he was there, brushing their coats to a sheen, picking the mud from their hooves, or tacking them up to go for a hack. He had a natural talent and an intuitive connection with the horses.

But the horses, along with everything else, were left behind when Paul fled Algeria. He was too busy in the decades that followed to follow that passion.

Finally though, with the Château built, and the business growing, Paul, who was now in his fifties, had the capacity to turn part of his attention to his twin passion. It was the late 90's, and at last he could realize his dream of having his own horse farm, while still managing his vineyards and winery.

He started by building the barn. It was no ordinary barn. From the street it looked like a smaller version of his house, with red bricks and black shutters and a symmetrical design. This was no country barn made of grey weathered wood. The aesthetics matched the main house precisely. Inside several spacious stalls overlooked the perfect rows of grapes. The horses would have better views than most people. Beyond the barn, a bucolic pasture awaited. The paddock was huge, at least an acre. There was lush green grass for grazing, a picturesque rail fence, and a serene pond complete with a small island. The picture was just missing one thing—a horse!

Soon after the barn was built, the first occupant arrived.

It was no ordinary horse.

For years, he had been researching horses. He was enamoured of Arabian horses—not just any Arabian horses, but the rare Egyptian Al Khamsa Arabian horses. They were originally bred by desert Bedouins, and thought of as particularly pure. Only two per cent of registered Arabian horses in North America are Al Khamsas.

His plan was to breed this breed of horses. He was no less thorough in his research and pursuit of excellence when it came to horses than he had ever been when it came to viticulture and winemaking. He would shoot for the stars.

Through his connections with judges and experts, Paul became aware of an Al Khamsa Arabian stallion named Simeon Shai. This horse had made headlines in 1991, when he became the only stallion ever to win the Scottsdale Champion Stallion, the Canadian National and United States National Champion Stallion as well as World Champion Stallion at the Salon du Cheval in Paris, France, all in the same year. When Paul heard that Simeon Shai was at a ranch in Sierra Nevada, he and Paul Jr. headed to California. It was a beautiful ranch. Simeon Shai had been put out to stud by then, and was worth millions of dollars. Paul figured his pedigree was worth his stud fee of $5,000, and decided to breed a horse of his lineage. He arranged for a local mare to breed. Simeon Shai's semen was delivered by Fedex, the mare was bred, and the colt she delivered became Paul's first horse at his new barn.

He was a beautiful bay horse, with the characteristic concave dished face of an Arabian, and a long black mane draped over one side of his neck. He had big gentle eyes, and a sweet personality. Paul called him Eddie, and hoped to show him. But the day came when a local judge, who was very renowned, came to look at Eddie and assess his showing potential. He broke the news that Eddie wasn't quite a chip off the old block, and he wasn't material for the show ring. Those shows are really beauty pageants, so any small imperfection was a disadvantage. Eddie never became the champion Paul had dreamed of, but Paul loved him still. Eddie's sister Serena came to the farm as well. Paul ended up with 6 horses, exactly the number he had always planned on.

It was a working horse farm. Having horses in the vineyard was practical as well as a passion. Their manure and soiled straw was composted and used as natural fertilizer. Paul loved to patrol his vineyards on horseback, checking out bud break in the spring, making sure the leaves were pruned correctly over the summer, and tracking the progress of veraison as the grapes ripened on the vines in late summer. He was literally closer to the crop on horseback than he could be in a vehicle.

Paul had a horse trainer and coach named Richard, who was at the farm most days.

Paul and Richard would ride every morning, around 11 o'clock. They would make their rounds on horseback, riding first around the estate vineyards that surrounded the barn and Paul's home on York Road. Then they would cross the road, and ride to the back of the Château, around 11:15 each morning. It was deliberately timed, because at 11:15 there was always a group tour underway at the back of the Château. Their arrival on horseback was an instant wow with the tourists. They all wanted pictures with the horses, and they were so impressed to meet the owner of the winery in person. It was great P.R., that's for sure. Paul always got a kick out of it. This routine went on for many many years.

Paul Jr. rode with his dad sometimes, and helped take care of the horses when his dad was away travelling. Paul Jr.'s wife Michéle was quite a horsewoman, and spent even more time riding with Paul, until her back had issues that forced her to give it up.

Paul loved the connection he had with his horses, and the connection they had with his vineyards. His horses gave him great joy and pride every single day. So it was a dark day when his trusted trainer, Richard, pleaded with Paul to give up riding his beloved horses. Paul was 73 by then, and Richard felt his reflexes just weren't what they had been. The horses were well trained, and well behaved, but horses could be unpredictable if something startled them.

Richard was afraid Paul could be seriously injured if he had a fall. It was a heated exchange. It broke Paul's heart, but he realized Richard was right, and he reluctantly gave up riding.

Paul never gave up his ambitions to breed a winner. He'd spend hours pouring over catalogues to select a stud. His efforts to breed one of his mares were ultimately unsuccessful, but he tried his best.

Nevertheless, he spent hours everyday with his horses, caring for them. He meticulously measured their feed and supplements, was very hands on with them, and he always personally did their last feeding of the night.

Paul's love of horses inspired the name that was given to his best Bordeaux wine.

Paul Jr. had noticed that proprietary names for wines were becoming popular in the late 1980's, so he was thinking about a name for their premium Bordeaux. That was in the early days of the internet, and one day he stumbled across the name Equuleus. It caught his interest. Equuleus is a small constellation, and in the northern hemisphere it is seen in the fall, at harvest time, so that resonated with him. In Latin, Equuleus means "little horse". In Greek mythology, Equuleus was the lesser known half brother of Pegasus. Paul Jr. liked the underdog aspect of the character. He brought the name to his dad, and Paul was delighted. He loved it immediately. They commissioned an artist to create an image for the label, based on a photograph of Serena, one of Paul's Egyptian Arabs. It became an enduring symbol of rare quality. The wine is only made in years where the quality of the grapes hits a very high threshold, usually one year out of three.

Wins for the Winery, and for Paul Personally

Once the Château had opened in the '90s, it became a popular stop for tour groups visiting from Japan. The tour companies would build up their enthusiasm on the bus. They told them, "We're here to see the world famous Niagara Falls, and then we have another attraction for you! We're going to go along the beautiful Niagara Parkway beside the river, and all the way to the old town of Niagara-on-the-Lake, where you'll be able to shop and have a look around. This is where they make the world famous Canadian Icewine, and it's a perfect gift to bring home. We will stop right at a winery where you can buy it." The Château was right there on York Road, on the way back to the highway, very convenient, and the only winery of its kind at the time. The tourists were wowed by the Icewine. They'd never tasted anything like it before. It was sweet and luscious, and it carried the romance of a Canadian winter in the story of how it was harvested. The tourists couldn't wait to buy some to take home. It was very popular, and it became an important revenue stream for the business.

One of Paul Jr.'s sales reps at the time, observed that Japanese tourists brought a lot of attention to Canadian Icewine in Japan. He reasoned it would be a hot seller for travellers at the international duty free shop at the airport. Paul Jr. immediately agreed, and proceeded to make his pitch to the buyer for the duty free store in Toronto. Her response was, "Why didn't I think of this! Of course!." So a section was created in the duty free store for Icewine. Château des Charmes was a pioneer. It was the very first Icewine sold in international duty free shops in Canada and the U.S. In addition to Toronto, it was in Vancouver, Calgary, Washington D.C., Las Vegas, and Denver.

The Ontario duty free stores were regulated by the provincial liquor board, and it had some very byzantine rules. The LCBO ruled that duty free stores could only mark up their wine by 25%. Oddly enough, this had a kind of boomerang effect that resulted in a huge profit margin for Château des Charmes. Since the markup was relatively low, the duty free store preferred to pay a higher price, and in turn charge a higher price to consumers. They got more revenue that way. So Château des Charmes raised their price by $100 per case, and the duty free sold it at a higher price point than it would have been at the LCBO. Paul Jr. customized the packaging, so it was consistent with the brand, but unique to the duty free shop.

The operator of the stores changed over the years, but the buyer remained the same, and she and Paul Jr. became friends. He and his dad would entertain her and her husband at the winery, and Paul Jr. would drop whatever he was doing if she wanted to see him in Toronto. The profit margin went up to 300 or 400% per unit. They sold thousands and thousands of cases. It was by far their largest Icewine market. Those were the glory years, financially, for Château des Charmes, and they came at the right time. They had borrowed millions from the Bank of Montreal to build the Château earlier that decade, so this windfall allowed them to reinvest and pay down on that debt.

Unfortunately, the party didn't last forever. Château des Charmes had blazed the trail, and created a new category in duty free stores, and eventually others noticed. While they had had it all to themselves for the first four years, that was about to change. Vincor, which owned Inniskillin and created Jackson Triggs, was a huge entity. It reasoned that there was an opportunity to make a mark with Inniskillin Icewine. As a large company with resources at its disposal, it could ramp up production at Inniskillin. Vincor made the capital investments for new presses and hundreds of acres of vineyards to be netted. They arranged for the participation of many farmers to grow and harvest the grapes. That decision paid off for them, as Inniskillin became easily the best known Canadian brand of wine around the world. Its Icewine eventually became available in 50 to 60 countries around the world.

The duty free store didn't kick Château des Charmes Icewine out, but they did say it was time to share the shelf space. The game changed, and the margins shrank, but Château des Charmes was still making money, just not as much. 25 plus years later, their Icewine was still in the duty free store in Vancouver, but no longer in Toronto.

Opportunities can swell and fade in business. The duty free story is just one example. Another sales win for Paul Jr. was with Air Canada. Château des Charmes had its wine on Air Canada for several years in the late 80's, after Paul flew to Montreal several times and secured that sale. It was a lucrative deal, and allowed him to reinvest in stainless steel tanks that would eventually find their way into the cellar once the Château was built in the 90's.

Paul Jr. got the opportunity to revive the presence of Château des Charmes wines onboard Air Canada some 15 years later, in 2003. The process was different the second time around. Renowned wine critic Tony Aspler had recently written a glowing review of a vintage 2000 Château des Charmes red Bordeaux blend, and he gave Paul Jr. the heads up that Air Canada was putting together a panel to taste through a lot of wines to choose the next wine to be featured on the airline. Paul Jr. submitted that wine to the panel, knowing it was far from a sure thing. There were more than one hundred wines being tasted. At that point, the wine had to stand up for itself. Paul Jr.'s charm and salesmanship alone couldn't win the day. The stakes were high, because the wine would be poured in business class. Not only would it be a big sale, it would be tremendous exposure to a prestigious market. Château des Charmes beat the odds, and the wine won out over all those others! Paul Jr. made sure the wine was always delivered on time, and he managed the relationship with Air Canada over the next three years. Over that time, they sold more than 20,000 cases of wine to Air Canada. It was revenue in the realm of seven figures, a big, big boost to the winery. It came at a time when they really needed it, because two major events had had a catastrophic effect on tourism. 9/11 had happened back in 2001, which curtailed tourism and travel for a time. Then there was the SARS crisis in Toronto in 2003. It happened during the summer. The message to the world was, don't go to Canada, it's the epicentre of SARS. So the visitor season was ruined that year, in particular Asia Pacific tourism, which was a lucrative channel for selling Icewine right at the winery. The profit from direct sales was much higher than selling it through other retailers.

In addition to the needed revenue, the Air Canada sale built reputation. Paul Jr. heard from people time and time again, "I just had your wine on my Air Canada flight, it was great!" The flights were often long, so passengers had lots of time to see the bottle, and read the label. The website was on the label, so the winery used to get lots of emails from passengers complimenting them on the quality of the wine, and asking if it was available in their home province. The deal was commercially successful. It was very important in terms of money, but the exposure and brand building opportunity was really second to none. And it was all on the shoulders of Paul's winemaking and visionary viticulture.

Paul never felt like that was the end of his struggles though. He felt his feet were always to the fire, and challenges would continue. It wasn't the sort of business, and Paul wasn't the sort of man, to say 'well we've made it!'

Order of Canada

Opening the Château was a watershed moment for the business, and those big deals with duty free and Air Canada had buoyed the business in the years that followed, but on a personal level, Paul had an exceptional honour on the horizon. On November 18, 2005, Paul was named to the Order of Canada.

When Paul saw the letter saying he was going to be an Order of Canada recipient, he was incredulous. His reaction was subdued, but he was exceptionally moved.

The event itself was a star studded affair. The Governor General was Michaëlle Jean, who was very glamorous. Shania Twain was invested the same day! At the dinner, Paul and Andrée were seated beside Hilary and Galen Weston. She was Lieutenant Governor of Ontario at the time, and Paul was very taken by her. Paul Bosc Estate Cabernet Sauvignon was on the menu. What a heady night!

That honour meant the world to Paul. Whenever he went anywhere, he wore the pin proudly on his lapel. He wouldn't draw attention to it himself, that wasn't his style. He preferred if someone noticed and commented on it. He described himself with humility, saying that he had always worked hard, been persistent, and was never a quitter, qualities he carried from his life in Algeria to his pioneering role in the Ontario wine industry, and his successful enterprise.

Paul may have been 70 years old, but he saw neither his age nor his accomplishments as signals to slow down. He still had much to do!

Part Four

Into the Future

Serendipity, Named Amélie.

Paul's passion for experimenting in the vineyard never faded, even after he had established his vineyards and proved he could make consistently excellent wines. He always had a block of vines with a wide range of different varieties, always testing to see which were best suited to the soil and the climate in Niagara. At least one friend remembers seeing Paul walking that vineyard and talking to the vines. He was deeply connected with the soil and the life it brought forth. This same quality had been part of who he was since he was a child, and it sustained and drove him throughout his career.

As he entered his seventies, Paul was still very much in charge. By then, he knew for certain that his second son, Steph, would not be taking over as winemaker. He had groomed Steph to succeed him in the cellar, but family business isn't for everyone, and by then Steph had left the business with finality.

Paul had three people working directly for him. Dr. John Paroschy had joined Paul in the 80's as a researcher. He had a doctorate from the University of Guelph and he worked under Paul's direction on the viticulture development and research side. There was also a winemaker with an assistant. The model was very much command and control, with Paul at the apex. It worked very effectively that way, but as the years rolled by, everyone was getting older.

By 2011, Paul himself was 76, and he had some health issues. Dr. Paroschy was in his sixties, with retirement looming. The winemaking team was fine under Paul's hands-on supervision, but he didn't see them as successors to his legacy and family business. The question of who could take over if something happened to Paul was never far from the surface. He was acutely aware of the clock ticking.

It was a troubling situation with no apparent solution. There had been a few summer interns at the winery over those years, but none made an impression on Paul. He wouldn't hire just anyone to cultivate the vineyards and winemaking he had poured his heart into. He needed someone special, someone who understood his exacting passion and precise techniques for the vines and the soil and the cellar where the grapes were crafted into wines worthy of his name.

Paul and Paul Jr. didn't know it as the calendar marked the beginning of 2011, but three thousand miles away, at the University of British Columbia, something was percolating. Perhaps the stars between Niagara and Vancouver were coming into alignment. Strands of serendipity began to weave together. The seeds of this circumstance were sown years before.

Back in 1996, the Cool Climate Oenology and Viticulture Institute (CCOVI) was born in Niagara, as a partnership between Brock University, the Grape Growers of Ontario, and the Wine Council of Ontario, to focus on research and education. The new institute wanted a renowned expert to head it up, and it recruited Hennie van Vuuren, an acclaimed PhD oenology researcher from South Africa. He was welcomed with great fanfare, as CCOVI got on its feet. Not surprisingly, Paul was very supportive of CCOVI and the work it was undertaking. It dovetailed with the pioneering work he had been doing for decades. He would often entertain Dr. van Vuuren and other CCOVI colleagues at the winery, and the two men got to know each other, and respect each other well. But there was disruption ahead. van Vuuren received an offer to go to UBC to become the founding director of the Wine Research Centre there, and he chose to accept it, less than two years after starting at CCOVI. Industry leaders in Niagara were devastated that their star player was leaving so soon, but it turned out to be the right decision for van Vuuren.

Fast forward more than a decade, and van Vurren, still at UBC, had a promising student working in his lab. Her name was Amélie Boury. She was from France, and was studying viticulture, oenology, and biotechnology there. Amélie came to UBC to do her engineering internship at the Wine Research Centre under van Vuuren for six months. After that internship, she went back to France to finish her degree, and graduated at the top of her class in oenology. She had been studying for seven years, and she wanted to get to work. Amélie had loved her time at UBC, and wanted to go back to Canada, so she asked van Vurren if he knew any established wineries where she might be able to work and learn. She had been one of van Vuuren's top students. She was highly effective in his lab, very dedicated, and very likeable. He remembered Paul from his time in Niagara. van Vuuren knew that Paul placed great value on all things French when it came to technology and know-how. He thought Paul and Amélie would make a good fit. He told Amélie, "you should contact the Bosc family. I remember that winery, it was quite extensive even back in the days I was there. Paul Sr. does a lot of research, and he's very passionate about it." Of course, research was Amélie's passion as well. Things unfolded quickly from there.

Van Vurren called Paul Jr. and told him about Amélie. They had a long chat. van Vuuren said he could guarantee that Amélie was a great winemaker, and he told Paul Jr. that he thought of the Bosc's first. When Paul Jr. relayed the conversation to his dad, Paul cottoned on right away.

Amélie, meanwhile, was keen to pursue the lead, so she sent Paul a handwritten letter, not knowing what to expect. Before she knew it, she got a call from Toni, who was Paul Sr.'s personal assistant. Toni said, "Mr. Bosc would like to talk to you." Amélie was a little taken aback in the moment, but Paul came on the line and they talked for more than an hour. They just clicked right away. They loved talking about the science of viticulture and winemaking. They were fellow wine nerds who had found their kindred spirits. Amélie was so excited. This was in the Spring, just before she graduated, in May. More phone conversations followed, and by August 1, 2011, Amélie was on a plane to Toronto. Well laid plans for her arrival went awry, though, and before she set foot in Niagara she found herself wondering what exactly she'd got herself into.

Amélie's flight was scheduled to land in Toronto shortly after Paul Jr. was due to land there on a flight from Calgary. The plan was for Paul Jr. to meet Amélie when she arrived. He had told her, "You'll be looking for me, go to the website, my picture's on there. I'm that guy, I'll be waiting for you as you come out." Except, he wasn't waiting for her when she came out. Paul Jr.'s flight from Calgary was delayed. Significantly delayed. He had no way of getting hold of Amélie to let her know what was happening. She was alone at Pearson airport after a long flight, already exhausted, and now stranded. Amélie had the wherewithal to figure out what was happening. She knew Paul Jr. was coming in from Calgary, so she realized his flight was delayed, and waited. It wasn't a short delay, it was three hours. Finally Paul Jr. arrived. By then it was super late, after midnight. The airport was deserted. They left for the hour-plus drive to Niagara. Amélie was bone tired as they drove toward Niagara. When they approached Hamilton, and the car climbed over the Burlington Skyway bridge spanning the industrial harbour, her eyes widened in alarm at the eerie spectre of smokestacks and blue and orange flames from the steel mills casting an ominous glow into the night sky. "Where am I and why did I come here?" she wondered wearily. Amélie wanted to come to Canada after her experience in Vancouver, where she loved the natural beauty of the mountains and ocean and old growth forests. Hamilton harbour came as an unpleasant surprise, especially as seen in the dead of night.

It was after 1:30 in the morning when Paul Jr. dropped Amélie off at the apartment he and his wife Michéle had rented for her. It was in a house on Warner Road, near the winery. Amélie may have been feeling some trepidation at that moment, but Paul was wide awake in his house, waiting like an excited kid on Christmas morning. They'd had hours on the telephone talking, but he couldn't wait to meet her. When Paul Jr. got to his own house after dropping Amélie off, his phone rang. He was groggy, but he answered. It was his dad. "Dad, why are you calling me at this hour?" He just wanted to know about Amélie. All Paul Jr. wanted was to get some sleep, but his dad was persistent. "What's she like?" he wanted to know. "Dad, let me get some sleep, I'll come over later this morning, or this afternoon. But I will say this, I don't know how much she knows, you'll have to find that out, she'll be working more closely with you than with me. But I can see opportunities to work with her. She's cute as a button. She's the real McCoy." With that, Paul Jr. hung up to get some much needed rest. His dad had to wait a little longer.

Paul Jr. and Michéle helped Amélie get settled in, and get her bearings for a few days. Michéle took her grocery shopping, and showed her around. She met their son Alex, who was five years old at the time. Paul started showing Amélie around the vineyards. Harvest was about to start three weeks later, so she had to quickly settle and get used to things, and get to know the team.

The Boscs had taken care of the immigration paperwork, clearing the way for Amélie to work there. She had a one year contract, reporting directly to Paul. They sat down one day and Paul said, "Well, you know, once the year is closed, we will sit down and see how things are going." Amélie happily agreed. Her intent was to spend a year there, and then travel to Australia for another year and then travel around more.

Paul became Amélie's mentor. They started with the winemaking, which she knew most about, and then he taught her about the vineyard after that. In oenology school she had learned about the vineyard, but it wasn't really hands-on like the winemaking was. Once Amélie was comfortable understanding the nature of the terroir and how it was translating in the wines, she was ready to explore what was happening outside in the vineyard. Paul was exacting in his methods and lessons. "We don't cut any corners," he insisted. "No cutting corners in the wine cellar, and no cutting corners in the vineyard." It was a lasting lesson.

Paul was somebody that wasn't always easy to approach. People were maybe not scared of him, but he could be intimidating. He wasn't interested in spending time with anyone who wasn't truly interested in the vineyard, but for anyone with passion and a desire to listen and learn, he opened right up. He was like that with Amélie from day one, and he never tired of helping her learn and develop. In turn, she soaked it up, and never had any trouble with his direct way of speaking.

One of Paul's own mentors was an expert from Bordeaux in France. Paul studied his books and picked his brain whenever he could. This mentor told Paul that he had observed that the oenology students who did the best were the ones that came from farms. That added something to their ability to transition from the academics of oenology into the real world, and those were the students who stuck to it. Others would go to wine school and then go and do something else. But the students with a farming background were the ones to stay and succeed. That always stuck with Paul, and it was one of the reasons he believed in Amélie from the start. She grew up on a farm in France, not far from the Belgian border. They grew grains and mixed crops, and livestock. Paul respected that grounding.

As that first harvest season unfolded, Thanksgiving came and Amélie was invited to the family home for Thanksgiving dinner. She felt welcomed and included in the family from the beginning. She and Paul became like a grandfather and granddaughter to each other.

That first harvest season was a whirlwind, but Amélie dove right in. She contributed to the team from the beginning, even as she was learning more and more. The first year passed quickly, and as it came to a close, Paul and Amélie sat down together. Paul said "it's working out for us, I'm really happy with you and I'd like you to stay. You have a bright future here." Amélie said, "Initially, that was not my plan. But I'm very happy here and I'd like to stay." Paul promised to do everything that had to be done to ensure she was able to stay. He hired an immigration lawyer and paid for everything, and she got a new work permit.

That was 2012, and the two continued working together. In 2014, Paul made Amélie Director of Oenology, her first big title, and she was working without anyone above her. Two years later Paul promoted her to vice president of Winemaking and Operations. Three years after that her responsibilities expanded to include viticulture too, and she became vice president of Vineyards and Winemaking. At the same time, Amélie had become the public face of Château des Charmes, representing it at winemakers dinners and industry events.

In addition to the daily demands of the winery, Paul and Amélie were always working on the experiments. They established criteria for the plants, and for the wine she made with them. They would narrow down which vines performed best, and which to weed out. The promising ones were eventually planted on a larger scale, to give a better idea of how they fared.

In the vineyard, Amélie found if there is one thing that she could say, it is that if you've made wine in Ontario, you can make wine anywhere in the world. Nothing is by the textbook in Niagara as it changes so much. Some years everything would go well through the growing season, and she would have so much hope it would be one of those great years. Then September comes and boom! Everything goes tilt if the weather isn't good. She and her team worked hard all year, because they knew those great years make amazing wines. They took meticulous care of the vines, and she made good wine every year in spite of varied conditions. She relished those years when the weather was her friend. It took very hard work and dedication.

When the vines were dormant, in the off season, Paul would go to the trade shows in France. He took Amélie with him on three occasions, in 2014, 2016, and 2021. They would focus on viticulture, visiting vineyards, and focussing on new technology. They would look at tractors and barrels and such. The second time they were in France it was in December, and they went to a Christmas market. The tables were loaded with traditional sweets. *Pates de fruit*, which were candied and jellied fruits, *calissons*, which were biscuits flavoured with melon and topped with marzipan, walnut tarts, mandarins and cherries. Paul was diabetic, so it wasn't an ideal spread for him to feast from. But he was insistent on stopping, and when he did, it triggered stories. He told Amélie about how his grandmother made lemon coffee, and he loved all the familiar flavours he remembered from family reunions at his grandparents farm in Algeria. He said to Amélie, "My grandmother, she used to make quince jelly, do you know what quince is?" And she said "Yes, not a lot of people know what quince is or what it tastes like, but I do." It was one of Amélie's favourite moments. It was what food and wine do, particularly for Paul and Amélie, because they would taste something and it would trigger stories that could go on for hours.

Later, when she would go to France on her own, she would always bring back candied fruit rinds. She always told him not to eat them all at once, but he usually did anyway. It was maybe his one weakness. He was otherwise very disciplined about his diet.

Paul was ill with diabetes and kidney disease for the first few years that Amélie knew him. He got a kidney transplant in 2015, and he was one of the oldest patients ever to have a kidney transplant at McMaster Hospital in Hamilton. His health and wellbeing improved dramatically after that, but he had to take care of himself. He was always extremely regimented when it came to taking care of his health. He was very conscientious and a model patient. That's why the transplant was so successful.

The last trip that Paul and Amélie took to France together was in November 2021. It became a tale to tell. By then, he and Amélie were very close. The morning they were going to leave for the airport, she checked with him to make sure he had everything he needed to take on the plane and on the trip. "Do you have your transplant documents, do you have your nitro, did you pack a needle in your carry on?" she asked him. "Yes, yes, yes," he replied. And off they went to the airport.

They boarded the flight, and all was well. Three hours into the flight, though, who does Amélie see approaching her seat, but Paul. He was sitting in business class to give his legs room to move, because his circulation wasn't great. "Amélie!" he said. "I can't find my needles for my insulin." Amélie asked him, "How are you feeling?" He said, "I just checked my blood sugar, and hey, it could be okay, but it might not be okay. I don't know." Amélie took a deep breath. "Ok, let's not panic," she said. Then a flight attendant came over to them. Paul had asked her, before he went to Amélie, if they had any needles in their CPR kits, so she knew the situation. She checked, and couldn't find a needle. On the announcements, the crew asked if there was a doctor on the plane. The flight was soon to head straight over the Atlantic ocean. Amélie went to see Paul in his seat up front and asked, "My god, is that about you?" He said, "Yes, but I think they're becoming a bit dramatic. They're telling me they want to land the plane." Amélie went to ask the flight attendant what was happening. She confirmed they were planning to land the plane. The next thing she knew, there was an announcement on the intercom. "We have a medical emergency on board, so we have to land the plane in Halifax. We can't cross the Atlantic with this patient without getting medical attention." Passengers started grumbling immediately, but there was no turning back. The plane landed, and the paramedics came on board to take Paul off the flight. "You're not taking me anywhere. I'm not leaving. I'm going to Paris!" he insisted. "Just give me a needle, all I need is a needle!" He was adamant, and the paramedics were no match. They administered an insulin injection, and left the aircraft. The plan had to refuel though. It sat on the tarmac for two or three hours. The other passengers were fuming. Their connecting flights were all messed up. They arrived in Paris in chaos, not knowing how to re-organize their flight to Bordeaux. Paul and Amélie went to the Air France booth to sort it out. Paul looked back at the lineup of anxious travellers all trying to resolve their own plans, and said to Amélie, "Look at the chaos I've created," with an almost evil laugh. And that was just the beginning of the trip!

Things turned around after the disastrous start. They went to the trade show, and Paul had a chance to visit with one of his best friends. Then they were off to Paris. Paul knew it was the last time he would be there, so he wanted to see all his favourite landmarks one more time. He was 86 at that time. They went to some of the best restaurants in the city. For Amélie, it was a very, very good time sharing that experience with him. At the same time, it was very funny because Paris was nothing like he remembered, and he thought the changes were for the worst. He'd say, "What do you mean we can't walk there anymore? What do you mean the cars don't drive there anymore?" and so on. The visit was full of great moments and great stories, and for Amélie it was very personal.

Back at the winery, Paul was still fully engaged in what was happening in the vineyards and the cellar. Long after Amélie had assumed full responsibilities for all aspects, he would be out there, and always in touch. It wasn't that he was checking up on her, it was more that it was what he loved. He would call her, and say, "Oh, did you see this?" Or, "You should come here, I want to show you something."

Amélie and Paul had a very close connection, and that was the only way it could work. He was so passionate about it all, he couldn't have transitioned anyone into that role unless they were truly aligned, especially in the family business. It was as important to Amélie as it was to him, and it was seamless between the professional side and the personal bond.

Bidding Adieu

After that last trip to France with Amélie in 2021, Paul continued to be active in the vineyard and at the winery, but he was secure in knowing the winery was safe in the hands of Paul Jr. on the business side, and Amélie on the wine side. That didn't mean that harvest season would come and go without Paul walking the vineyards and watching over the grapes as they came into the crush pad. He was never far from the action, and he always had a question or a suggestion.

The family had lived through the untimely death of Paul Jr.'s wife Michéle in January of 2019, and the sadness of losing Madame Andrée in March of 2021, but life went on. The winery struggled through the pandemic as did the entire industry. By 2023, tourist traffic was growing again, though it hadn't rebounded to pre-Covid levels, and the winery continued to evolve, with an eye on increasing events like weddings, building on the direct to consumer online sales that had spiked during the pandemic, and concentrating on the highest quality of wines.

Paul was experiencing some health issues in the summer of 2023, so he went to his doctor, who arranged for some tests. He was still driving himself into Hamilton where the hospital was. In fact, on one trip home, he was pulled over for speeding, but, ever charming, he managed to talk his way out of a ticket. Paul went to see Paul Jr. as soon as he got home that day. He couldn't believe what he'd been told. He'd been diagnosed with lung cancer. Paul was indignant. "I haven't smoked for 35 years! That's crazy, how could I have lung cancer!" he exclaimed to Paul Jr. that day. All his life Paul had been a self proclaimed fighter. He never accepted defeat in the face of a challenge, and this was no different. He was determined to fight the illness, and proceeded with the treatment plan. He continued to be an active part of the business. As summer melted into fall, Paul was having more and more trouble staying mobile. But that was no barrier to still making his contribution to planning future projects.

One day there was a meeting scheduled with bankers at the winery. Paul wasn't able to walk over that day, so the meeting was simply re-located to Paul's dining room table at his home across the road.

That meeting with bankers was part of a long process of negotiation to sell Château des Charmes. He and his son had decided that it was time, recognizing that Paul Jr. didn't want to run it alone. It had always been a family business, a team effort, but Paul Jr.'s wife had died five years earlier, and Paul's own wife passed away just two years ago. He was fighting for his health, but they both knew he wouldn't be around forever. It was time to pass the torch. They found a buyer they thought would be a good fit, and discussions were well underway.

Paul may have been very ill by then, but he hadn't lost his taste for special sweets. In November, Amélie went to Toronto to see some friends for her birthday. She went to a French store there. They had those special sweets Paul had loved at the Christmas markets in France, the candied fruit and jellies. Amélie bought some to bring back for Paul. She went to see him, and said "I brought you these sweets." Right away, he started telling his stories again, about his grandmother, and the coffee and quince jelly she made. For Amélie, it was a bittersweet moment that became one of the best memories of Paul she would have. They shared that bond of the tastes of food and wine, and the meaning they had. Paul was almost 90, but those flavours still sparked vivid memories from his childhood that he loved to share.

That was just a couple of weeks before Paul died. He eventually ended up in hospital. Paul Jr. and his son Alex kept vigil at his bedside. Paul was no different in death than he had been in life. He was never one to give up easily. The doctors predicted he would pass away within a day or two, but Paul lived on several days longer. He died with his son and his grandson by his side, and his legacy was certain to live on.

When news of Paul's passing became public, the accolades poured in. Long time wine writer Tony Aspler said, "His legacy is written across the vineyards of Niagara and beyond, He was really THE pioneer of vinifera in Ontario." "He put Gamay on the map in Canada, and today it has blossomed," from wine critic Michael Vaughan, who also said "Paul was a master winemaker and he knew it all started with the grapes." From Donald Triggs, himself an industry pioneer, "Paul's vision on vinifera viticulture opened the doors for our industry. He brought a foundation on which our industry prospered." There were many many more, all in the spirit of honouring his innovation and passion in the vineyards and the wine cellar.

His son Paul Bosc Jr. was at first philosophical about his father's passing, focussing on his gratitude for having had so many years with him, and reflecting on his fathers' contributions to the industry and his indestructible perseverance. In the months that followed though, Paul Jr. felt the loss keenly, and missed being able to share moments of joy, or just everyday events with him. Their relationship was so close personally, and they were partners in the winery, right to the end.

Two memories that Paul Jr. especially treasured had to do with his father and his son Alex.

Just a couple of summers before Paul died, Amélie was supervising the re-planting of vines in the vineyard behind Paul's house. The original vines there were more than 40 years old, and it was time to replace them. The whole vineyard crew was out there working, and so was Alex, who was being treated no differently than the other workers. Like his father Paul Jr. before him, Alex's summer job was working at the winery. Paul came out to see how it was going, and he saw Alex there. He reacted with a mixture of surprise and pride. There was emotion in his eyes as he watched his grandson renewing the vineyard he had planted four decades earlier. Later that summer, Alex spent many weeks in the cellar working with the winemaking team. Paul Jr. was there the day that Paul came down to check on what was going on. There was Alex, wearing big rubber boots, his clothes sprayed with grape juice and water.

He was a mess, which was an occupational hazard. Paul was visibly moved, seeing his grandson working hands on, making wine in the cellar he had built. It had been 60 years since Paul had fled war ravaged Algeria, not knowing what his future held, and there was his grandson, the third generation of his family, making wine in his own family winery.

In the few last weeks before his death, Paul's mind reached back in time, remembering those days before he left Algeria. He kept a photograph of his mother on his bedside table. She had died just before he left Algeria, when he was only 27. She had been a formative force in his life, and her influence on him continued as he built his new life with his family in Canada. His eyes rested upon her face as he slipped in and out of sleep over those last weeks, his beloved cats Coco and Minou curled up behind his knees. He reflected on the long road that had been his life, the many challenges, the hard work, the accomplishments, and the satisfaction of seeing his legacy taken up by his son, Paul Jr., and his grandson, Alex.

When Paul Bosc Sr. died on December 2, 2023, he was 88 years old.

The Next Chapter

The long negotiations that had begun before Paul's death continued after it. Paul Jr. and his father had been determined to find the right buyer for the winery. They didn't want to sell to just anyone, not to a large corporation, nor to foreign buyers. The group they found seemed to be a perfect fit. The new CEO would be Marco Piccoli, who, like Paul Sr., got his formal wine education in Europe. Paul of course studied in France. In Marco's case, it was Italy and Germany. Once in Canada he had a long career as a winemaker at Arterra, which owned both Jackson-Triggs and Inniskillin wineries. Marco knew and respected Paul and his legacy. He partnered with Anne Givens, who had had a long and successful career at such prestigious international wineries as Mondavi and Rothschild, and subsequently a very senior sales and marketing role at Arterra. Paul Jr. knew and admired them both, and valued their Niagara roots. On the financial end was an investor who lived in Southern Ontario, and by chance, (or fate?), had had his wedding at Château des Charmes some years earlier. It took a long time to dot the i's and cross the t's, but by early summer the deal was done. Paul Jr. kept the property across from the winery on York Street, with the house his dad built, the barn and the horses, and 43 acres of vines. Part of the deal was an agreement that he would sell the grapes from the vineyard exclusively to Château des Charmes for 10 years.

The new owners took possession of the winery, the 72 acres of vineyards, and the brand in the summer of 2024. Amélie stayed on as winemaker, continuing Paul's practices in the vineyard and the cellar.

Anne and Amélie decided to inaugurate a new tradition for their first harvest season together. It harks back to an old practice in France, where the beginning of harvest season is celebrated with the whole community coming out to help pick the first bunches of grapes. Both Anne and Amélie had experienced the joyfulness of the harvest celebration in France, and they wanted to kick off their own harvest season that way.

So early one September morning, before 7:30, a crowd of eager people gathered in the sunshine to celebrate the first day of the harvest at Château des Charmes, and to make their own contribution by hand picking grapes destined for sparkling wine. There was a buzz of anticipation and excitement as the coffee and pastries were offered. Then it was into the vineyard, orange handled clippers in hand, to pick ripe clusters of Chardonnay grapes. Amélie led the way, demonstrating proper clipping technique, a warm grin on her face. Everyone was smiling or laughing as they dropped the bunches into the bins, from youngsters to seniors and all ages in between. It was the first harvest at Château des Charmes since Paul had passed away, and it felt like his spirit was present as the golden rays of the bright sun shone down and the joy of a good harvest filled the vineyard. As it turned out the whole harvest season of 2024 was picture perfect, some say the best ever. Perhaps it was a gift from Paul's spirit to those who had assumed stewardship of his beloved vines.

Marco was in the vineyard that morning, and he watched the scene from a slight distance as it unfolded. He was reflecting on the junction the winery was at, and how that would guide him as the still-new CEO and President. He had known Paul personally, and had great admiration for him and for the legacy he had left. Marco saw the transition as a generational passing of the baton. It was his responsibility to honour the iconic brand that Paul had built literally from the ground up, while taking Château des Charmes to what he thought of as the next level. To Marco this was a normal state of affairs, it was exactly how things happened in Europe. Whether wineries remained in the same families or not, there was always a handing off from one generation to the next, and a tradition of abiding by the core values, but stepping firmly into the future with shifts in winemaking styles, or production practices, or marketing priorities. The wine industry is dynamic, and has always needed to evolve to meet the market even as it held true its origins. As he watched the hand harvesting of grapes destined for the winery's fine sparkling Blanc de Blanc, it reinforced his vision for the future.

For Marco, the vision was clear and simple. It would build upon the Bosc family foundation, which had always been based on uncompromising quality, from the vineyard to the cellar to the bottling line. To him, the natural extension was to zone in on sparkling wine and Icewine as luxury items. Château des Charmes already made excellent traditional sparkling wine as well as Icewine, so elevating both wasn't a stretch. Luxury was a category where the consumer was headed, and where Château des Charmes already shone. It had great potential to shine even brighter, through marketing, placement in ritzy hotels and restaurants, and expressions in hospitality experiences at the Château itself. The wines would be chic, they would be present in elegant venues, and be integrated into classy 5 star events. It wasn't a change in direction, it was an amplification of what was already there, and it was tailored to shifting consumer demand. Consumption of wine, and alcohol generally, had been declining. But a luxury wine would be part of a special experience that consumers would be willing to pay for. Wine has such deep traditions. Even with reduced overall consumption, Marco believed a great dinner or a special occasion would always call for an excellent glass of wine. When you've paid $40 a pound for a nice piece of steak or $50 for a fresh lobster, it's okay to spend $80 on a fine bottle of wine. Not every bottle has to hit that standard, people can still enjoy something less expensive. The focus on luxury would not be to the exclusion of the other great wines in the portfolio, but luxury would lead the way.

Paul Jr. provided guidance in the early days of the transition, but soon shifted gears to focus on his own future and new projects. Though the winery was sold, he still had the estate vineyard across the road from it, with 43 acres of vines, 3 horses, 2 cats, and his fathers' home. After his whole life supporting his father, selling their wines, and his long tenure as CEO at the winery, he had now morphed into a grower, selling his grapes exclusively to Château des Charmes. It was a strange feeling after that first harvest, when he went to Vineland where the Grape Growers Association was handing out cheques to growers from the wineries that had purchased their grapes. It was a long established practice that the wineries that bought grapes gave the money to the Grape Growers Association to disburse to the growers. Paul used to be on the other side of that equation, but now those tables were turned.

Caring for that vineyard of course was a key priority for Paul Jr. He still remembered planting many of those vines. He also had some other endeavours in mind. He started straight away on two projects he'd been planning for some time. One, was to build a residence to house the seasonal workers who travelled from Mexico every year to work in the vineyards from March until November. Most had been working for the family for many years, and they were very skilled and reliable. Paul Jr. was building a beautiful building to house 16 workers, symmetrical in design and clad in red brick just like the Bosc family home. It was set well back from York Road to be away from traffic and noise. It was much more expensive to do it that way, but like his father, Paul Jr. wouldn't compromise on quality. There was nothing like it in the region. Paul hoped it might inspire others to provide a similar standard of living space to workers at other vineyards. At the same time, he was constructing a very large barn on the property. Tractors and other farm equipment could be stored there, and repaired as needed.

His son Alex was on the verge of starting university, and Paul was ensuring he would have a choice to stay in the family business in its new iteration if he chose to, while understanding it would be a choice to come in the future. It was not a foregone conclusion. He planned to renovate and update his parent's home, but that would wait until the new buildings were complete.

Change had come, and would continue, but it all rested on the foundation that Paul Sr. had built, and not just the foundation for Château des Charmes. He had been a force among that small cabal of vinifera rebels back in the 1980s, the innovators who established the bedrock that the modern wine industry in Niagara rests upon today.

Looking Back, Looking Forward

Paul Sr. was a key leader in the early days of what has become the modern wine industry in Niagara, which has the largest acreage of vineyards in Canada. He and a small band of innovators pushed and pulled and persisted. Eventually others adopted vinifera grapes, making quality wines, and adhering to standards set through the VQA. Their wineries had been risky ventures in those early days, as they gambled on their vineyards and cellars, and hoped they could convince consumers to embrace their wines. Most of them made 500 cases from their first vintages, and now they produce in a range from 20,000 to 60,000 cases each year.

Some of those first wineries have since changed hands, but they are all still producing fine VQA wines. Inniskillin merged with Cartier in 1992, and later became part of what is now Arterra; Marynissen and Lailey wineries were sold to new owners in 2012 and 2015, respectively; while Cave Spring, Henry of Pelham, Reif, and Konzelmann remain in their original families. Reif is available for sale, but only to the right buyer. Klaus Reif doesn't have a family heir for the business, and wants to have more time to spend with his aging parents and for leisure. Allan and Brian Schmidt are still respectively President and Winemaker at Vineland Estates, which has been owned by Fred DeGasperis, of construction fame in Toronto, and the DeGasperis Family Trust since 2004. Château des Charmes was sold in 2024, although Paul Bosc Jr. retained the estate vineyard across from the winery, and the grand Bosc family home.

The industry has grown exponentially from that original group of nine plus the six large wineries back in the 80's. There are 194 wineries in Ontario as of 2025, dominated by the two biggest players, Andrew Peller Limited and Arterra. They each own several estate wineries which make VQA wine. In Peller's case, it owns Peller Estates, Trius, Gretzky's, and 30 Bench in Niagara, as well as several others in British Columbia. In the case of Arterra, their portfolio includes Jackson-Triggs, Inniskillin, Le Clos Jordanne, and Kew winery as well as various international brands. Arterra is huge, with roughly a 60-65% share of the International Domestic Blend (IDB) market in Ontario, and 40% of the VQA share. Peller is increasingly focused on VQA quality wines, though IDBs still comprise a healthy chunk of their overall sales.

Virtual wineries are a category on the rise. There have long been individual winemakers who operate in a virtual manner. They make wine by sharing facilities with established wineries, and sell their wine at other wineries, to restaurants, and online. The most notable of those is celebrated winemaker Thomas Bachelder, known for his premium, terroir driven burgundies. He's been making wine under his own name for many years, and is also the winemaker for Le Clos Jordanne which reopened in a new permanent location in 2024. Derek Barnett, renowned for the excellent wines he made at Lailey, created his own brand, Meldville, after Lailey was sold in 2015. Rennie is another virtual brand, made and sold out of Malivoire Winery for years. In 2022 Graham Rennie became one of the founders of a new collective of independent wineries under one roof, called Niagara Custom Crush Studio. It boasts modern production facilities and a retail space where independent wineries can create and sell their brands. There's a second collective for virtual winemakers called Collab Wine and Beverage, which operates in partnership with Marynissen winery. Both Crush and Collab allow small operators to produce and sell their own wines without the usual barriers to entry, namely huge capital investment in vineyards and facilities and regulatory expertise. These producers add another layer to the landscape, with their small lot production and passion driven offerings.

Niagara has been called Napa North by some, and the winery landscape is very similar, if on a vastly smaller scale. Like California, Niagara's wine ecosystem comprises very large corporate wineries, along with many small to medium sized boutique operations, and some very small artisanal producers. Some are still owned by the original innovators, some are owned by those who have made their fortunes in other arenas and turned to owning a winery as a hobby or passion project, and some are owned by people simply with a passion for wine.

Taken together, the collective critical mass helps with consumer awareness, and provides a united front to lobby the government for more favourable regulations and taxes. The larger wineries have provided key leadership on that front, in concert with the smaller operations. The variety of operations offers consumers a wide range of wines, and provides tourists with many different experiences. Wine tourism to Niagara wine country draws 2.6 million visitors a year. It's a far cry from the days when Madame Bosc would welcome occasional weekend visitors to the cinderblock building on Creek Road and offer them a tasting, or Mrs. Lenko would offer homemade apple pie in her kitchen to visitors! Yet those were the roots from which the bustling wine tourist trade grew from, and it keeps on growing.

The Ontario wine industry now has an economic impact of $5.49 billion each year, and supports 22,000 jobs. *(source: Wine Growers of Ontario)* VQA production supports 15,125 of those, because the wine, by law, is made from 100% Ontario grapes. International Domestic Blends (IDB)supports a lower number, less than half, at 7,260, since it's made with up to 75% imported wine. That rule changed in the spring of 2025, so the IDBs will only be able to use 50% imported wines, which is expected to increase demand for Ontario grown grapes.

In terms of annual sales, VQA wines account for $433 million as of March 2025. *(source: VQA)* Roughly half of the grapes grown in Ontario are used for VQA wine, and half for International Domestic Blends. Marketing studies have determined that VQA and IDB consumers are quite distinct from each other. IDB shoppers are motivated by affordability, and buy IDB wines to drink casually at home. VQA shoppers are willing to pay more for wine, and tend to buy VQA wines for social occasions.

The environment today is entirely different, with extensive investments in infrastructure to support the industry, including excellent education programs at both Brock University and Niagara College, and innovative research at CCOVI (Cool Climate Oenology and Viticulture Institute), and Vineland Research Centre. Recent changes in provincial regulations now allow for expanded retail sales with access to grocery stores across the province. Now wineries can hire well trained winemakers and viticulturists. When they started, they had to hire where they could and teach the people they hired on the job. In the early days at Henry of Pelham, Paul Speck was hiring people who'd been laid off when General Motors closed down. They didn't even drink wine, let alone know anything about making it. It was a new day when the training programs started. The current head winemaker at Henry of Pelham, Lawrence Buhler, was among the early graduates of the viticulture and oenology program at Brock, in 2003.

Rapidly changing conditions will force all to adapt, as challenges and opportunities abound. Climate change is a wild card, as extreme and unpredictable weather patterns pose existential threats. Retail modernization to allow wine to be sold in grocery stores and other outlets presents a great opportunity for expanded distribution, but also could increase competition for Arterra and Peller who are the only ones who own their own off-site retail outlets. Consumer habits are changing, with levels of consumption decreasing. Various impacts may materialize as a result of the trade war unleashed by U.S. President Trump. Interprovincial trade barriers are dropping, which could give Ontario wines access to more markets across Canada. A nationalist buy-Canada sentiment has fuelled greater sales of Canadian wines. The removal of U.S. wines from LCBO shelves has significantly boosted sales of Ontario wines, so more Ontarians have discovered local wines. Whether they'll stick with them when the U.S. wines return to the shelves is unknown. Tariffs could hurt exports, and the economic risk of recession could hurt sales, if consumers have less disposable income to buy wine. There are many variables in a constantly shifting environment.

Running a winery has never been for the faint of heart, or for those who seek instant gratification or sure fire profit. They're vertical enterprises, with the complexity of dealing with everything from the vineyard to the cellar, to all the ins and outs of marketing and sales and government regulations. Any number of things can go wrong at every step of the way. The current wine industry has become a significant economic driver and proud cultural force, routinely winning international awards. Still, it's a struggle to remain profitable, especially for the smaller wineries. Of those with annual sales under $5 million, less than half of them, a mere 45%, report making a profit. Of those with annual sales over $5 million, 88% are profitable. Those with sales over $10 million, are all in the black.

Ontario's wine industry has long been buffeted by various forces, and waves of change are surging over the landscape. Even as uncertainty looms, today's winemakers and entrepreneurs have a solid foundation beneath their feet, and the deep passion that propelled the pioneers to meet past challenges, will support today's wine growers in their determination to meet the future.

Epilogue

A Tribute by Wine Writer Tony Aspler

When Paul Bosc Sr. died in December 2023, Jill Troyer wrote an obituary in *The Lake Report* newspaper.

For her column, she asked me if I would like to make a comment on his passing.

I wrote: "His legacy is written across the vineyards of Niagara and beyond. He was really THE pioneer of vinifera in Ontario."

Now that I have had the time to reflect on the loss to his family and to the Canadian wine industry—and have been offered the space to elaborate my thoughts—I would like to expand on that quote.

As the wine columnist for the *Toronto Star* for twenty-one years, I had followed the career of Paul Bosc Sr. since 1980, two years after he founded his own winery. I was aware of his 15 years as winemaker at Château-Gai and his commitment to planting only the noble European varietals when the industry was still working with North American hybrids, like Seyval and Baco Noir. I recall a wine he made in 1975 from Gamay which Château-Gai labelled Gamay Beaujolais.

A fifth-generation winemaker from Algeria by way of France, he was the first Canadian winery owner who held degrees in oenology and viticulture (from the University of Dijon in Burgundy) and came with the experience of growing wine in both France and his native Algeria.

Bosc's first winery in Niagara was an unprepossessing cement block bunker set in the vineyard. Eventually he would build a winery worthy of his accomplishments and his ambitions – a palatial Loire-style Château with an imposing family home across the road.

There was a sense of grandeur in the winery as you enter the main door and see the curved staircase and the well-appointed tasting room on the ground floor. With his late wife Andrée and his son Paul-André, Paul Bosc Sr. created an impressive portfolio of wines in the French style supplied by fruit from his four separate vineyards.

Along the way he introduced several new varieties to the province—Aligoté, Viognier and Savagnin; and from his original vineyard a new clone of Gamay which he called Gamay Droit. (Droit is French for upright or erect.)

I recall visiting the original winery in the early 1980s and Paul took me into the vineyard. He showed me a single Gamay vine that towered over the rest. 'I'm going to propagate that vine,' he said, and the rest is history.

Paul Bosc had a long affiliation with the National Research Council to undertake research projects covering many oenological avenues such as carbonic maceration, clonal selection, reverse osmosis, vine performance relative to tile drainage, new canopy management techniques and climate control through the use of wind-machine technology.

His love of horses—he bred Egyptian Arabians—was commemorated in the name he chose for his flagship red wine, Equuleus—a Bordeaux-style blend made only in the best years.

Equuleus is Latin for 'little horse' and the name of a small, faint constellation in the northern sky, representing a little horse or foal in Greek mythology.

Acknowledgments

My heartfelt gratitude goes to Paul Bosc who shared his life stories with forthright generosity and wry humour. His son Paul-André shared his own stories as well, and filled in the gaps for me. He was always available and he patiently answered every question I brought to him.

Winemaker Amèlie Boury recounted her relationship and experiences with Paul, who mentored her from the day she arrived at Château des Charmes. She conveyed their mutual respect and fondness with tales both tender and funny.

Renowned wine expert Tony Aspler became my own mentor and friend. He read my early drafts, and made many valuable suggestions and comments. Tony connected me with Mosaic Press, and publisher Howard Aster nudged me to make the book better. His astute guidance was sharply focused but wrapped in kindness.

Many people in the wine industry, particularly those who were part of the "vinifera rebels" contributed so much. Thank you to Len Pennachetti, Paul Speck, Allan Schmidt, Klaus Reif, Donna Lailey, Debi Pratt, Albrecht Seeger, and Mattias Oppenlaender.

On a personal note, thanks go to my best friend Helen who could see the end at the beginning, and to my husband Don, who was my sounding board through the ups and downs along the way.

Thanks to Paul Bosc Jr. and Amélie Boury for their photos.

PHOTO: DON REYNOLDS

About The Author

Jill Troyer lives in Niagara-on-the-Lake where she is immersed in her twin passions of writing and wine. She has won more than 50 awards for her journalism, both in broadcast and print. Jill has completed WSET3, an advanced, internationally respected Wine Education program, and she writes about the Niagara wine industry for *The Lake Report*.